IN SEARCH OF
FAITHFULNESS

WILLIAM E. DIEHL

IN SEARCH
OF
FAITHFULNESS

*Lessons from the Christian
Community*

Fortress Press   **Philadelphia**

Biblical quotations, unless otherwise noted, are from the Revised
Standard Version of the Bible, copyright 1946, 1952, © 1971, 1973
by the Division of Christian Education of the National Council of the
Churches of Christ in the U.S.A., and are used by permission.

COPYRIGHT © 1987 BY FORTRESS PRESS

Library of Congress Cataloging-in-Publication Data

Diehl, William E.
  In search of faithfulness.

  1. Christian life—1960–.   2. Faith.
I. Title.
BV4501.2.D499 1987   248.4   87–45318
ISBN 0–8006–2064–X

3006C87   Printed in the United States of America   1–2064

Dedicated to
HILDA

CONTENTS

INTRODUCTION

For the past twenty-five years there has been great concern that mainstream Protestantism has been in a malaise. To compare the zest and vitality of the early Christian church with that of traditional Protestant congregations today is to compare growth and decay. Whereas the first-century Christians were part of a movement that ultimately penetrated every nation and class of people in the world, twentieth-century Christians have become virtually invisible in today's world. Membership in mainstream Protestant denominations has scarcely kept pace with population growth and, in many cases, is actually declining.

Despite a strong resurgence of activity within evangelical Protestantism in recent years, there is little evidence that the conservative movement is reshaping American values and priorities in any significant way. One has the uneasy suspicion that the evangelical movement has really been taken over by political conservatives who wish to press forward their own agendas while dressed up in Sunday clothes.

One looks in vain for evidence that American Protestantism, either mainstream or evangelical, either corporately or through its members, is exerting any lasting influence on this nation's political, social, or economic institutions. Yet the church of the twentieth century proclaims exactly the same message and mission as the church of the first century.

What has happened to the Christian faith? Why is Christian faithfulness virtually invisible in American society today? Where are God's faithful people? What do they look like? This book will answer these questions.

I have been in business for forty years, most of them spent in various levels of management in a major corporation. More recently, I have been doing management consulting with a variety of corporations. I have learned a great deal about the American economic system and I have developed many skills which have enabled me to compete successfully in that system. I understand the importance of excellence and drive in order to succeed in the marketplace. I am at home in the world of business.

During those same forty years, I have been actively involved in various structures of the church, at both national and local levels. I have learned a great deal about the teachings of the church and I have grown in my faith experiences. I understand the importance of living in a faithful relationship with God in order to experience life in the fullest. I am at home in the world of religion.

For much of my life, however, those two worlds did not connect and, in some respects, they still stand apart. There were times when it seemed as if I were two different people. Yet, the more I have matured the more I have come to believe with a passion that my relationship with God inevitably and directly relates to every aspect of my life. My experience is not unique. It is common. As I have discovered in the writing of this book, not only business people but persons from all walks of life, who identify with the Christian faith, find great difficulty in connecting their world of religion with their other worlds of occupation, community, and family.

In the past few years, there has been a steady stream of books dealing with success in business. Ever since *In Search of Excellence*[1] became an instant national best seller in 1982 a plethora of other books have emerged, dealing with both corporate and individual success and excellence in the world of business. Since business is one of my worlds, I have been reading those books. What began to dawn upon me as I read one book after another was that none of them made any mention of religious values held by business people. Neither the corporate values established within excellent companies nor the personal values held by successful business leaders seemed to relate in any way to the Christian faith. At least, no connection was stated.

Why? Was it that business and religion are such worlds apart that it makes no sense at all to mention the one within the realm of the other? Was it that those who write business books are not equipped to deal with issues of the Christian faith? Is there a fear that it will be offensive to the reader of a business book to make any mention of the religious values or convictions of business leaders? Is it an embarrassment to mention religion in the world of business?

On the other hand, I have found that current writers of religious books have very few kind words for the business community. Most business executives I know are convinced that our religious leaders have a strong bias against the free-enterprise system and, in particular, against large business corporations. When theologians such as Michael Novak or Robert Benne do write a book in defense of democratic capitalism, they are generally castigated by large numbers of other church leaders who accuse them of selling out to mammon.

Why is this? Is it that those who write religious books are not equipped to deal with issues of the world of business? Is there a commonly shared belief that the arena of business is so full of evil that it is beyond redemption? Is it an embarrassment to speak kindly of business within the religious community?

If very little good about religion can be found in the world of business and very little good about business can be found in the world of religion, how in the world can business people be Christians and vice versa? Are the business people who worship in church on Sunday frauds or hypocrites or schizophrenics? Can God's faithful people be found in an environment that worships success?

If one tried to discover God's faithful people in the world of business, how would one begin? Is there any difference between a faithful person in business and one in teaching, or farming, or homemaking? What is faithfulness in any arena of life? How do we identify faithful people? Just what do we mean when we talk about faithfulness?

This book is about the search for faithfulness. I decided to look for faithfulness in those very places where it appeared not to be—in the world of business, for instance. And I decided to use exactly the same approach used by Peters and Waterman in their best seller, *In Search of Excellence*. In their search for excellence among business corporations, Peters and Waterman first had to define excellence. They did so by interviewing many people in business to see how they defined corporate excellence. The authors then established their definition of the term.

Having defined excellence, Peters and Waterman surveyed many people and conducted additional interviews to discover which companies best fit the definition of excellence. As a final step, they carefully studied the "excellent" companies to determine if there were certain attributes that seemed to be common among them. They discovered eight attributes of management excellence that were commonly found in excellent corporations. These were described in some detail in succeeding chapters of the book.

In Search of Faithfulness uses exactly the same approach. First, the need to define faithfulness. To do so, we interviewed many Christians from all walks of life and surveyed the writings of a number of Christianity's best-known theologians. From these sources, we were able to give faithfulness a definition that would be the basis of subsequent work.

Our second step was to ask many people to describe those persons whom they have known who meet the definition of faithfulness. We talked about those people and listed the attributes they had, the practices they followed, and the values they cherished. Out of these interviews and an extensive survey done among business people, we have been able to identify seven attributes or marks that seemed to be found in some degree among all faithful persons. These seven marks of faithfulness are presented in some detail in succeeding chapters.

But another question emerges: Why is it necessary to *search* for faithfulness? Why is it not more obvious? Why do contemporary movies, books, plays, magazines, and television have so little to say about the faith lives of people? Why is it that the religious dimension of American life is presented almost exclusively by religious organizations themselves, through the media of their own publishing houses and radio and television stations? We believe we have found answers to these questions and, in doing so, we have discovered a rather shocking fact: The church itself is the principal barrier to faith development among its people. For a variety of reasons, which will be discussed later, it is the church which is primarily to blame for the fact that all the "excellence" books make no mention of religious values or beliefs among business leaders. The church actually frustrates spiritual growth and faith development among its members. In addition to showing how this happens, this book also offers suggestions as to what can be done to correct the problem.

In Search of Excellence carries the subtitle *Lessons from America's Best-Run Companies.* For reasons stated above, this book carries the subtitle *Lessons from the Christian Community.*

Christian faithfulness can be defined and observed. God's faithful people share many attributes in common, but the twentieth-century church must do much better in nurturing growth in the faith. Only then will Christianity reclaim the dynamism and zest of the earliest followers of the Way.

ONE

IN SEARCH OF
FAITHFULNESS

American business people do not believe in God. Or, if they do, it is certain that religion plays no role in their daily lives. This is the inescapable conclusion one comes to after reading the multitude of "excellence" and "success" books that have been cramming the shelves of bookstores in recent years.

The instant success of Peters and Waterman's *In Search of Excellence* spawned a plethora of books with similar themes. *In Search of Excellence* dealt primarily with studies of America's best-run corporations and the factors that contributed to their success. One of the eight factors was values. An entire chapter is devoted to values; in it many corporate leaders are quoted regarding their value systems. Not once in that chapter, nor in the entire book, is any mention made of religion, church, God, the Bible, or any other terms commonly used by churchgoing people.

Capitalizing on the success of his first book, Tom Peters quickly teamed up with Nancy Austin to produce *A Passion for Excellence* in 1985.[1] Under a subtitle of *The Leadership Difference*, the authors set out to describe the day-to-day acts of leadership at every management level. Again, in 425 pages devoted to business leadership, there is no mention of religion, God, the Bible, the Ten Commandments, the golden rule, or anything of a remotely spiritual nature. In one chapter there is a fleeting reference to Dr. Martin Luther King, Jr., as a "symbol." In the same chapter there are sections devoted to "love" and "empathy." But again, with absolutely no mention of religious or spiritual values.

It is not simply the trait of one author. I have surveyed *Executive Success*, edited by Eliza G. C. Collins,[2] *Creating Excellence* by Craig R.

1

Hickman and Michael A. Silva,[3] *Managing for Excellence* by David L. Bradford and Allan R. Cohen,[4] *Rogers' Rules for Success* by Henry C. Rogers,[5] and *Management Excellence* by Heinz Weihrich.[6] None of them, not one, refers to the religious convictions, values, or practices of business people. Nothing.

A recent issue of *Fortune* magazine featured a lengthy special report on "The Year's 50 Most Fascinating Business People,"[7] assembled by most of the editorial staff. Each profile went into great detail about the business and personal life of the subject. Not only did the reader learn of each person's successes and failures in business but also of their hobbies, marriages, personalities, and character. In all sixty-four pages, the word "Christian" or "church" did not appear once. Two of the personalities, Ronald Perelman, chairman of Revlon, and Alan Greenberg, chairman of Bear Stearns, were identified as being Jewish. Greenberg was cited for being New York City's largest individual donor to the United Jewish Appeal, while Perelman was credited with keeping a strictly kosher household although "he refuses to discuss his religion." Harwood Cochrane, former owner of Overnite Transportation Company, gave part of his sixteen-hundred-acre home to the Southern Baptists for a missionary training center, but there was no indication in his article that he was a church member. In the profile of Drew Lewis, former Secretary of Transportation, there was a report of his receiving an honorary degree from his alma mater, Haverford College, which has a Quaker background. And, finally, there is a passing reference to Robert Campeau, a Canadian real-estate developer, being a "devout" Roman Catholic. That was it. Hardly a positive report on the religious values and convictions of some of America's best-known business personalities.

Forbes magazine tried valiantly to prove that, in spite of recent business scandals, the leaders of the country's largest business corporations are especially committed to religion. One hundred leaders were surveyed and, of those who responded (and the author did not give us the percentage), 65% said they attended church regularly. This participation in church services was compared to the 40% of the entire American population who claim to attend church regularly. Apparently the author did not consider the possibility that, of those who did not respond to a survey on religious practices, the level of church attendance could be significantly lower. Barbara

Kallen also reported on a number of business persons' Bible study and prayer groups known to exist throughout the country as further evidence of religious concern. On the other hand, Peter Grace, well known for his leadership of laypersons in the Roman Catholic Church, says about it all, "You call all these takeovers going on today 'religious'? There is no thought given to people's security, their families, length of service, the loyalty they show. I think the whole business community today in the U.S. is more heartless and less caring than it was when I first went to work."[8]

While some efforts have been made to connect religious belief with business life in book form, they have generally been initiated by members of the academic community. *Business, Religion and Ethics*, edited by Dr. Donald G. Jones of Drew University,[9] was a collection of eighteen essays, some written by business people, on the relationship of religion and ethics to business. The essays, however, really dealt with the relationship of religious institutions and their leaders to business institutions. Little mention was made of the role of the individual religious person within the business institution. Similarly, Oliver Williams and John Houck edited a collection of essays for their book *The Judeo-Christian Vision and the Modern Corporation*.[10] These essays, based on a conference held at Notre Dame University in 1980, also primarily deal with institutional and philosophic issues. The University of Notre Dame Joint Committee on Business, Theology, and Philosophy is illustrative of the types of initiatives that have sprung up in many academic circles. Conferences are held, representatives of the business community attend, papers are published, and generally the business world could not care less. As an avid reader of current top-selling business books, I have yet to find a copy of the Jones or the Williams and Houck books on the shelves of the major bookstores catering to business people.

It would be wrong to suggest that this situation represents a personal bias against religion on the part of the authors of the many success books. I am sure they are reporting what they are observing and they are observing .no intimations of religious or spiritual influences in corporate suites. A recent survey report of the American Management Association confirms that the success books are accurately reporting what they see. In 1984, the AMA released its report on *How American Chief Executives Succeed*.[11] Seven hundred eleven American chief executive officers (CEOs) participated in the study.

They represented a wide range of corporations—in size, nature of business, and geographic location. The designers of the survey first conducted a series of personal interviews with a representative number of CEOs to determine the kinds of questions that would go into the survey. Among the questions was, "What were the key influences in helping you to become successful?" The CEOs were able to come up with twenty-one possible "key influences." None of them, not one, had any hint of a spiritual, religious, moral, or ethical influence.

When the survey was completed, in first place among "key influences" was "a need to achieve results." Number twenty-one was "changing jobs at regular intervals." In between were a wide variety of job-related influences. A few of them might cause some academic ethicists to raise their eyebrows a bit, such as "a determination to get to the top ahead of others," or "an ability to develop more ideas than my other colleagues," or "an ability to make 'deals' and negotiate." Within a healthy competitive environment, those influences may indeed be positive ones but, in the wrong environment, they can be destructive.

But another pair of questions in the survey was even more revealing. In one instance, the CEOs were asked to name the activities they felt were most important in their making it to the top. In a companion question, these same CEOs were asked to list the activities responsible for the success of *other* CEOs. Among the fifteen attributes listed for other CEOs were "honest, compassionate," and "fair." *None* of these three appeared on the list where the CEOs evaluated *their own* success. The obvious question: Why do CEOs feel attributes such as honesty, fairness, and compassion help others achieve success but not necessarily themselves? Could it be that we define success one way for ourselves and another way for others?

I am a management consultant. I have five shelves of books dealing with principles of management, organizational structures, corporate culture, and the like. These books consistently avoid any reference to religion. They touch on such personal traits as social behavior, style of dress, relationship with family, involvement in politics, and personal habits. But nothing about religion. Religion simply does not play a part in the lives of persons in business. Or so it would seem.

PERSONAL EXPERIENCES

This was borne out for me throughout the thirty-two years I was with Bethlehem Steel Corporation. Except for occasional references to a church function, there was almost no meaningful conversation among my associates on matters of our faith. There were only two occasions that I can recall when religious issues were the focus of a conversation with an associate.

The first was when, as a salesman, I attended a business meeting in Washington, D.C., with several other salesmen. Following a day of meetings, three of us were having dinner. During the course of conversation, one of my colleagues, Ray, mentioned that Billy Graham was having a rally at the baseball stadium that evening. He asked if we had ever heard Billy Graham. I said that I had twice and I described the circumstances. Ray became quite interested and asked us to go to the rally with him. We agreed to do so.

At the stadium it became apparent that Ray was being moved by the stirring oratory of Dr. Graham. And so, when it came time for the "moment of decision," Ray looked at both of us and said, "Let's go!" John thought he meant he wanted to leave. I knew differently. "Ray," I said, "I'm afraid I just don't go in for altar calls." "Just go with me," he almost pleaded. He wanted to go down on that playing field but was afraid to go alone. "O.K.," I said, with some reluctance. When John discovered *where* we were going, he said, "Not me! Not in a million years!"

So Ray and I threaded our way through the crowd down to the playing field. Immediately two Graham volunteers approached us and began talking about our decision. Ray and I became separated and I explained to my volunteer that I was a Christian and had just come down from the stands to accompany a friend who was afraid to come alone. The volunteer understood immediately and I was permitted to stand to the rear of the "converts," waiting for Ray. When I next saw him, he had an armful of literature and was bubbling over with excitement. It was truly a conversion experience for him. So I tried to share that excitement with him as best I could.

For some months after that experience, Ray would phone me to ask if I had heard anything more from the Billy Graham people. When I said no, he would tell me of the latest materials he had received. Although he knew that I had not responded to the altar call the way he did, I was the only one he could share with. And so I did try to nurture him in his new faith even though I felt a bit uneasy about some aspects of the born-again theology.

The second occasion for a religious conversation involved one of our customers. I was manager of sales at the time and Bud was one of our smaller customers. I was aware of the fact that he had recently gone through a divorce, and that his company was operating under Chapter 11. He was living under very heavy pressure. One afternoon, I got a phone call from Bud. After a few preliminary exchanges, he blurted out, "Hey, I understand you are one of us!" "What do you mean?" I asked. "I understand you are a Christian, too!" he said with delight. "Well—yes, I am," I responded, not knowing where Bud was coming from. "That's wonderful!" he exclaimed. "Praise God!" He then went on to tell me of his recent conversion. "I've come out of the closet," he rejoiced. "I've turned over my company to Jesus Christ and things are now going great!" Then he added a shocker, "I hear you've come out of the closet also." I didn't know how to handle that. "Well, er—what do you mean?" "I hear you've written a book on *Christianity and Real Life.*" I acknowledged that I had such a book published about six months earlier. "Praise God!" he shouted. "You and I must get together and witness to each other." With some degree of uncertainty, I agreed that perhaps it would be good to share our faith stories sometime. We never did.

I learned a few months later that Bud had been found guilty of some illegal business practices and was sentenced to prison. The illegal activities predated his conversion, but, unfortunately, his new life in Christ did not impress the sentencing judge.

Those two events were the sum total of serious religious dialogues I had in thirty-two years of service at Bethlehem Steel. And in both cases I felt rather uncomfortable in my role.

There was one other occasion when *my* religious interests were used by my company to establish my character. It involved an antitrust suit brought against Bethlehem Steel. Since I was to be a key witness in the defense, our lawyers did a great deal of research into my background. When they discovered that I had been active for many years in my church and had recently authored a book on *Christianity and Real Life,* they were quite pleased. Such credentials, they assured me, would be quite valuable in establishing my credibility as a witness. And so, in the early questioning in the witness stand, considerable details were presented to the jury about my religious life. Again, I felt uncomfortable. My faith was being "used" by associates who never before had discussed religious issues with me. And, although they later established that my "highly credible" testimony was a key factor in winning the case, never again did we discuss matters of a religious nature.

One might well ask, "Well, Bill Diehl, what was stopping you from initiating your own conversations with associates?" In one sense, nothing; in a larger sense, everything. It simply was not part of corporate culture to talk religion. In the same way no one had to tell you not to wear tennis shoes to work, or forget to shave, no one had to say that religion is an off-limits subject in this corporation. We all knew it.

What is true in the realm of business is true in countless sectors of our society. My lawyer friends report that religious talk is off-limits in their profession, even in social gatherings among their peers. I get the same impression from talking to doctors, dentists, architects (except *church* architects), blue-collar workers, and government employees.

If someone from another planet were to arrive on earth and try to learn about Americans, based on their current literature, newspapers, magazines, movies, radio, and television, the visitor would undoubtedly conclude that within American culture there is a small subset of persons who produce "religious" books, newspaper columns, magazines, movies, radio and television shows, but that otherwise religion does not play a part in the lives of most of our people. Other than the TV evangelists, for example, or news reports about the pope or Bishop Desmond Tutu, one searches in vain for media programs portraying any faith dimensions in the lives of most people.

CONFLICTING EVIDENCE

Yet pollster George Gallup would have us believe otherwise. In his extensive 1984 report on *Religion in America,* he claims that nine out of ten Americans profess a religious belief. Seven out of ten are members of churches. Six out of ten report that they have attended a religious service in the past month.

In 1985, Americans gave $80 billion to charity. Religious institutions received the largest share of such giving with a total of $37.7 billion.[12] The average American donated more than 2% of income to charity.

What is going on? A significant percentage of those persons which Gallup reports as going to church and a large portion of those who have been contributing to religious institutions have to be business persons, lawyers, doctors, blue-collar workers, and the like. Yet, as one surveys the literature of the secular occupations in America— indeed, surveys almost any segment of our culture—one can barely find a trace of reference to things religious or spiritual.

This dramatic contradiction can largely be explained by concluding that Americans are basically dualists. They divide their lives between things sacred and things secular, between the spiritual and the material, between the soul and the body, and between Sunday and Monday.

THE IMPACT OF DUALISM

Dualism has plagued Christianity throughout its history. The heavy imprint of dualism in Greek thought had an effect upon the early Christian church. The medieval church, in order to preserve its eroding authority over the lives of its people, encouraged a division into sacred and secular. While its authority might be challenged in matters secular, there was no doubt about its authority in matters sacred. Luther's doctrine of the two kingdoms has been attacked by some as another example of dualism. The claim is that this dualism was the reason Christians in Hitler's Germany did not oppose his massacre of six million Jews.

Unfortunately for the Christian movement, our present religious institutions benefit from dualism in the same way the medieval church did. As long as life is divided into things spiritual and things material, our religious organizations have very little outside com- petition for authority in their realm of matters sacred. There is competition between religious organizations for support of the believers, true; and secular institutions do compete with the churches for the commitment of persons to their organizations and agendas. But when one speaks of the Christian faith, secular institutions concede that only the church has authority to speak.

Of course, Christian dualism in America is not as sharply delineated as its definition might suggest. The secular world is very much involved in such religious holidays as Christmas and Easter. Great commercial gain can be had from marketing religious books, songs, artifacts, and TV shows. The borderlines between church and state are constantly being probed. How far can the state go in legislating matters which some religious groups consider sacred? How far can the church go in pressing for legislation which may be largely secular in nature? The limits are constantly being challenged.

Nor can people as neatly compartmentalize their lives as the definition of dualism might suggest. While to speak of a Sunday-Monday gap is a catchy way of illustrating dualism, it is obvious to all that Sunday is not without secular activities. Nor are weekdays without prayer, Bible study, Christian social action, and worship. In fact, many committed Christians earnestly struggle to make their faith more a part of their daily lives. Some religious people maintain that since God created everything, everything is sacred. They see a unity in body and soul and find spiritual dimension in all things material. In short, they reject the principles of dualism.

But for most of us there does seem to be a division between things spiritual and things material. We find it easy to use the terms "sacred" and "secular." And we have very definite opinions as to the degree that sacred and secular institutions should relate to each other. Therefore, most readers of the recent "excellence" and "success" books are not at all surprised that no mention has been made of religious or spiritual values, even though those same readers would not be surprised to learn that many of the heroes of those books considered themselves to be committed to their faith. It is not expected for secular business books to get into religious issues.

Which brings up a major question: If secular literature and art are not portraying the spiritual dimensions of society, how *are* faithful people relating their religious convictions to their so-called secular activities? What does it mean to be a Christian in the field of business, or law, or education, or medicine, or homemaking, or public service? What do God's faithful people do in the secular world? Do they pray at their desks and work benches? Do they proselytize? Do they preach the gospel to their associates? Are they givers or healers or mediators? What are the marks of a faithful Christian?

In fact, what *is* Christian faithfulness? How is it defined? How is it identified? How is it developed? Are there attributes or practices which are common to the faithful?

And so I decided to go in search of faithfulness. First, I wanted to find out how Christians define the word "faithfulness." Then I wanted to determine how faithfulness can be recognized or identified in others. Finally, I was curious as to whether these "faithful" people had common attributes or shared common practices. For the answers to these questions, I went to the people, the faithful. As a result of over 70 interviews and a survey by mail of 174 business people, I was able to answer my questions. The results constitute the primary content of this book.

TWO

DEFINING
FAITHFULNESS

Paul Tillich begins the introduction to his book *The Dynamics of Faith* by stating, "There is hardly a word in the religious language, both theological and popular, which is subject to more misunderstandings, distortions and questionable definitions than the word 'faith'."[1]

With a warning such as that, one might question the point of devoting a chapter to defining faithfulness. Yet, if we are to search for faithfulness in the world, we have to agree upon what it is we are searching for. Tillich defines faith as "the state of being ultimately concerned."[2] Understand at this point, he is not talking about Christian faith specifically. He is defining faith generally. He points out that any faith places demands upon the faithful, but it also "promises ultimate fulfillment which is accepted in the act of faith."[3]

Our so-called Protestant work ethic is an example of Tillich's point. If we give our ultimate concern to the work ethic, it will, in turn, demand of us a commitment to a life of hard work. But it will also promise fulfillment in one's lifetime. For some this promise has been fulfilled; for many it has not. Tillich's explanation of the work ethic's failure to deliver on its promise would be that, in reality, the "promise" was a finite one (wealth, prestige, power, etc.) and that it never really could promise "ultimate" fulfillment.

Tillich maintains that every ultimate concern must express itself concretely. Faith must be experienced for, as he says, "There is no faith without participation!"[4] Because faith is experiential, Tillich maintains that "there is no criterion by which faith can be judged from outside the correlation of faith."[5] I cannot judge your faith to be valid or not, simply because I have not been a part of your experience of faith. Nor can you judge mine.

The people who were interviewed for this book were asked to define faithfulness, based on their own experiences. They were asked to describe the attributes and practices of people whom they judged to be faithful, based on *their own* definitions. While the reader of this book may not agree with the definitions and observations of faithfulness of some of the people who were interviewed, we need to remind ourselves that the experience of faith is a very personal thing which manifests itself in different ways with different people. Yet it is interesting to observe that among those who were interviewed and the classical theologians, there emerges a general agreement as to what does constitute faithfulness.

The German theologian Rudolph Bultmann devoted much of his life to trying to clarify the meaning of faith in terms that ordinary people can understand. He maintained that faith is not an abstract term. Rather, it is a personal commitment of an individual to God. This commitment brings with it a new self-understanding which is marked by a radically personal transformation. Bultmann is careful to point out that faith is neither defined nor attained by works. He makes quite a distinction between "acts" and "works." An act is something that involves one's whole existence—such as getting married. Works are things we do within the context of our acts. For example, assuming certain specific responsibilities within the marriage relationship are works. As will be seen later, many of the people interviewed describe faithfulness as being free, open, unafraid, and unshackled by the world. Bultmann likes to define faith *as* freedom. This theme is present in his books *Faith and Understanding, I,* and *Existence and Faith.*[6] He writes that faith is freedom from oneself, from the world, from the law, and from death. Faith is freedom *for* love.

Karl Barth, another of modern Christianity's most influential theologians, defines faith as "simply following, following its object. Faith is going a way which is marked out and prepared."[7] He relates faith and knowledge and maintains that unless knowledge grows, faith cannot grow. "Without an increase of knowledge," he writes, "there can be no increase in faith."[8] He is not referring to the assent to religious doctrines or theological constructs. Rather, he speaks of the need for knowledge of Jesus Christ as taught by the Bible.

The Danish theologian Søren Kierkegaard described a faithful person as one "who is willing to give up the dearest earthly things in obedience to God, and precisely in so doing rejoices in and affirms the earth and human relationships more passionately than ever before."[9]

Dietrich Bonhoeffer, who was executed by the Nazis in the Second World War and whose life has been an inspiration to many, said this about faith: "The fundamental reality of the life of faith is simply placing oneself at God's disposal."[10] If you are familiar with the life and struggles of Bonhoeffer, he did just that.

The brief review of how a number of classical theologians define faith and faithfulness illustrates that it can be viewed in a number of different ways. Care should be taken not to adopt a tightly drawn doctrinal definition of Christian faithfulness since it is a subjective matter. As Bultmann maintains, Christian faith can really be discussed only as "my faith" in any given moment.[11]

THE INTERVIEWS

To discover how people "of the faith" define and identify faithfulness, I went to approximately seventy persons, all of whom had at least a nominal relationship with the church, and asked some questions. About fifty of the interviews were conducted face to face. Approximately twenty were done through the mail. There were advantages and disadvantages to both means, I discovered. The advantage of a personal interview was that it allowed for feedback and clarification of statements made. On the other hand, in the face-to-face interviews the respondent had no advance notice of what the questions would be. Their responses, therefore, were generally spontaneous and without much prior consideration. In fact, many times during our conversations, a respondent would go back and modify the initial definition of faithfulness that had been offered.

It appeared to me that those who replied to my written request for their opinions gave a good deal of thought to the questions before putting their replies on paper. Their words seem to have been carefully chosen and generally a few paragraphs of explanation were provided for each question to ensure clarity. Yet, the problem did remain that I had no opportunity, in these cases, to ask follow-up questions for greater clarification.

By far, the best interviews were with those thirty or so persons who were asked to put their thoughts on paper, after which we met for a discussion of the questions. This provided time for some personal reflection and the careful drafting of a response and the opportunity for me to ask additional clarifying questions.

DEFINING FAITHFULNESS

Each interview was preceded by a brief explanation of the purpose of the book I was writing. I was very careful to point out that there were no preconceived "right" answers to the questions, but that I was trying to discover how the people of the faith define faithfulness. Three questions were presented.

The first question was, simply, How do you define faithfulness? In spite of the fact that my explanation of the purpose of the book indicated that I would be dealing with Christian faithfulness, a number of persons chose to define faithfulness as being loyal, reliable, trustworthy, steadfast, or dependable. When these persons were given a follow-up question on how they define faith, almost all of them spoke in religious language. If these persons were asked to define Christian faithfulness, they tended to use words such as "being true to God," or "having a commitment to one's God." One woman, a writer, objected to the term "Christian faithfulness." She asserted that faithfulness was constant in its meaning, and the adjective merely indicated what a person was faithful to.

But it is apparent that while the noun "faith" is clearly associated with one's religion by most people, the adjective "faithful" or the noun "faithfulness" is frequently used in more general settings. Some of the persons I interviewed, and they tended to be teachers and writers, objected to limiting an understanding of faithfulness to religious issues. Their criticism is valid. Should that criticism be honored by giving this book the title of *In Search of Christian Faithfulness?* Perhaps. But, because the book was being written about those who live within the Christian faith and is being published by a religious publishing house, it seemed somewhat redundant to me to be that specific in my title. After all, I reasoned, the writers of *In Search of Excellence* did not feel compelled to specify in their title that they were really dealing with corporate excellence. Checking the book jacket of the Peters and Waterman book, however, I discovered that they had added a subtitle—*Lessons from America's Best-Run*

Corporations. It was then that I decided to honor the objections of my writer and teacher friends by adding to this title the subtitle *Lessons from the Christian Community.*

By far, most of the persons I interviewed immediately defined faithfulness in terms of religious language. But within this large group there were two major distinctions. Simply stated, they have to do with beliefs and actions. A number of people define faithfulness as a belief in God or Christ. These persons, and they tended to be ones well trained in the teachings of the church, asserted that faith involves a relationship with God, or Christ, irrespective of what one does. This faith relationship, they said, is really a gift of God and is not the result of any human actions or works. For them, faithfulness is simply accepting the relationship established by God and living within it. However, as we got to the second and third questions of the interview, these persons did relate faithfulness to actions. Tillich's statement that "there is no faith without participation" seemed to apply to this group of respondents.

The group that focused primarily upon actions defined faithfulness as either following the example of Christ in one's life or else asking what Christ would expect them to do in given situations. Dave, retired from a small business, defined a faithful person as "someone who lives up to the standards of Christ and practices the golden rule." Jim, a senior vice-president of a major New York bank, wrote, "Faithfulness is devotion and discipline to the life and teachings of Jesus Christ. It is putting Christ first and specifically asking in one's life, over and over again, the question, 'What would Christ have done?' or 'What would Christ have me do?' " Helen, a homemaker, defined a faithful person as a "worker for Christ and one's fellow person; God's assistant." Gloria, a librarian, defined it as "one who tries to live everyday life as a follower of Christ."

A number of respondents combined the belief and actions views of faithfulness. Will, who owns a small business, used those precise words in his definition of a faithful person. He said it was one who had a "belief in Jesus Christ and backed it up with actions."

It is important to point out that people did not identify "faithful" others by their good deeds alone. As is perfectly obvious, non-Christians perform many deeds of giving and caring also. Not one respondent suggested that good works were the sole marks of the

Christian. In every instance, the good works were related to the awareness that the "faithful" person had, in some way, made a statement of belief. The person may have made oral or written statements that professed a belief in God or Christ. The person may have been part of a community of faith, may have been a part of a Bible study group, prayer circle, or Christian support group, or may be actively working within the structure of a religious organization.

At the same time, a number of persons volunteered the opinion that not all persons who are members of religious organizations would meet their definitions of "faithfulness." One person quoted Jesus when he said, "Not everyone who says to me Lord, Lord, will enter the kingdom of heaven , but he who does the will of my father who is in heaven" (Matt. 7:21–23). Many people agreed that churchgoing by itself was no indication of faithfulness.

FAITH AND WORKS

The relationship of faith and works has been an issue the Christian church has grappled with since its earliest days. The roots of the Christian faith are to be found in the Old Testament with its many legalistic requirements. While the Old Testament certainly does picture God as compassionate and forgiving, as the one who has called, delivered, and protected God's people, the requirements of the law weigh heavy. The pre-Christian theology of the relationship of persons to their Creator was one of having to merit the approval of God through obedience to his laws. The Christian theology, as articulated by the apostle Paul, was a radical departure from this. It was in his Letter to the Romans that Paul, the theologian, wrote, "For we hold that a man is justified by faith apart from works of law" (Rom. 3:28). Again, when he writes to the young church in Galatia, he says, "A man is not justified by works of the law but through faith in Jesus Christ . . . because by works of the law shall no one be justified" (Gal. 2:16).

Does this mean that if one accepts the faith relationship with God, one need not be concerned with one's good works? Not so, says James in his letter to the early Christians. He writes, "What does it profit, my brethren, if a man says he has faith but has not works? Can his faith save him? If a brother or sister is ill-clad and in lack of daily food, and one of you says to them, 'Go in peace, be warmed and filled,' without giving them the things needed for the body, what does it profit? So faith by itself, if it has no works, is dead. But some one will say, 'You have faith and I have works.' Show me your faith apart from your works, and I by my works will show you my faith" (James 2:14–18).

The Book of James is an interesting one to study. It almost did not make it into the New Testament. Among the Latin writings of the early church, James is not quoted or mentioned until the middle of the fourth century. Even then it was regarded with great uncertainty. In the entire letter the name of Jesus Christ is mentioned only twice, and then only incidentally. Moreover, the letter makes no mention of Jesus as Messiah, nor of the resurrection. Some biblical scholars support the thesis that the letter was originally a pre-Christian "Letter of Jacob," which was edited by some early Christian writer who was seeking to speak to the Jewish Christians who were having trouble accepting Paul's theology of justification by faith through the grace of God alone.

Martin Luther was especially severe in his evaluation of James. In his *Preface to the New Testament,* Luther concludes with these words, "In sum: The gospel and the first epistle of St. John, St. Paul's epistles, especially those to the Romans, Galatians and Ephesians; and St. Peter's first epistle are the books which show Christ to you. They teach everything you need to know for your salvation, even if you were never to see or hear any other books or any other teaching. In comparison with these, the epistle of James is an epistle full of straw, because it contains nothing evangelical."[12] Luther did not believe it was of apostolic authorship.

Luther's harsh evaluation of James must be seen in the context of his own life. As a young monk, he struggled desperately to achieve a feeling of worthiness in the eyes of God. He worked at it without success. It was the full realization of Paul's statement that one is justified by faith alone that caused Luther to have his own conversion experience. He later wrote, "Then I had the feeling that straight away I was born again and had entered through open doors into paradise itself."[13] This doctrine of justification by faith became one of the key pillars of the Reformation. One should not be surprised, therefore, that Luther would have such a low opinion of an epistle which is heavy with advice on good works.

What is the point of all this? Why should we be concerned about the differing explanations of faith and works offered by Paul and Luther on the one hand, and James on the other? The point is that even today Christians have differing views on the faith and works issue. At one end of the range of conviction are those persons who believe so fervently in the doctrine of God's saving action through the life, death, and resurrection of Jesus Christ that it becomes an almost exclusive driving force in their lives. Actions or good works are considered to be almost irrelevant to their relationship to God. They are accused of championing "cheap grace." At the other end of the range are those Christians who apparently have real difficulty accepting the gift of God's grace, without any merit of their own. These persons see Christ as the model of perfect obedience and strive mightily to be like him, yet always remain uneasy about whether they have been "good enough."

As I interviewed people for this book, their viewpoints on the faith-works issue ranged from one extreme to the other. When I asked questions about how one would decide that another person is faithful, many people concluded that it would have to be based on the person's actions. A smaller number of persons maintained that one cannot determine that another person is a faithful Christian based on his or her actions, since non-Christians do very fine works also. These persons concluded that a "search" for faithfulness is an effort doomed to failure.

For me there is a direct link between faith and works. I kind of resonate with Will who said faithfulness was "a belief in Christ and the action to back it up." I am not sure I would use the phrase "to back it up" but I do agree with the order. First, there is the belief *in* Jesus Christ. As humans, we can believe at different levels. We can believe *that* something is true or worthy without becoming involved in it. But when we believe *in* something which is true or worthy, we are a part of it. For example, one can believe that marriage is a fine institution without ever getting married. But if one truly believes in marriage as a fine institution, one is inevitably led toward the experience of marriage.

So it is with our beliefs related to Jesus. On the one hand, it is possible to believe *that* the theological principle of salvation through the sacrifice of Jesus is true without experiencing Jesus in our lives.

It is also possible to believe *that* Jesus was a wonderful teacher and role model without experiencing the assurance of God's unqualified acceptance of us simply through God's grace and without merit of our own. But when we believe *in* Jesus Christ, then it seems to me that we acknowledge the wonderful gift of God's grace in such a way that we experience the life and teachings of God's son, Jesus, in our own lives. God initiates a relationship with us in such a way that our acceptance of it immediately involves responsive actions. This relationship of belief and actions plays an important role in our search for faithfulness.

ELEMENTS OF FAITHFULNESS

As I read the various definitions theologians have given to the word "faithful" and as I listened to the words of persons interviewed for this book, there began to emerge certain elements that enter into the definition of faithfulness which will be the basis of our search.

First, there seems to be the *acknowledgment of God's faithfulness*. For one to live in Christian faithfulness there must be the acknowledgment that God is faithful in God's relationship with us. We must acknowledge that this relationship is a gift, freely given, without any merit on our part. Barth uses the word "acknowledgment" in describing the aspects of faith.[14] It is a good word. To acknowledge a message involves more than merely receiving it. It involves letting the sender know that it has been received. Acknowledgment involves response.

Second, this acknowledgment is not simply an intellectual belief. It is a *belief in* that relationship which automatically brings with it certain actions and behavior.

Third, since Jesus Christ was the means for revealing this graceful relationship we have with God, it is *Christ who is the model* for how our responsive actions should be patterned.

Finally, there is the recognition that any relationship is *dynamic*, not static. We are always *growing* in our relationship with God in the sense that our acknowledgment of the relationship continually deepens and our responses to it continually expand. Our relationship with God never reaches a final point in this life; it is constantly growing and maturing.

Just as the authors of the book *In Search of Excellence* had to come

to the point of defining the word "excellence," we have now come
to the point of defining the word "faithfulness." As it will be used
in the remainder of this book, *faithfulness is acknowledging God's
graceful relationship with us by striving to grow more Christlike in our
daily lives.*

Having thus defined the term, the question now becomes, Where
does one *find* faithfulness? Is it possible to identify faithful persons?
Are there beliefs, values, practices, and actions which are the marks
of faithfulness? To answer yes to these questions places one in a very
judgmental position, yet our study suggests that there are objective
ways of identifying faithfulness as we have defined it.

One thing is certain: Faithfulness, as we have defined it, cannot
be found without listening to people. Actions or good works alone
do not define Christian faithfulness. One needs to hear from a person
how he or she perceives the relationship with God. It is this self-
understanding of a relationship together with the manifestations of
that relationship that will lead us to find faithfulness.

But where and how does one find faithfulness?

THREE

THE SEARCH

In their book *A Search for Excellence,* Peters and Waterman conducted extensive interviews with sixty-two selected American corporations to see if there were common traits or attributes that contributed to excellence within them. In my search for faithfulness, I secured data from two primary sources: interviews with many persons within the Christian community and a survey of a particular group of Christians. The interviews will be summarized later in the chapter, but for now let us consider the survey.

THE SURVEY

First, a bit of background: For the past five years I have served as a consultant to the Lutheran Church in America's Center for Private Sector Affairs, which operates under the oversight of the Department for Church in Society. It has been one of my criticisms of Christian denominations that they invariably turn to government for the solutions to social problems. However, the private and the voluntary sectors of our society also have great potential for dealing with social problems, and the churches have done little to relate to the private sector in particular.

Therefore, my assignment with the Lutheran Church in America was to bring together church leaders and leaders from the private sector to discuss issues of social concern. One of the means for doing this was the creation of events and occasions in which business leaders would discuss a current societal issue with church leaders participating primarily as listeners. A Lutheran theologian was always a part of such conferences to provide biblical and theological perspectives to the issues being discussed. Over the years, we have had conferences dealing with the New Federalism, the de-industrialization of America, protectionism, the social impact of industrial change, the global economy, work and identity, television and the family, and others. The business leaders who have participated in these events have been high in their praise of them. "It has been the first time the church has ever called me into a meeting with other business persons to listen to what I am dealing with in my job," said a participant in our very first conference. His feeling has been echoed many times over.

It has taken us some time to develop a mailing list for these conferences. While religious organizations do try to identify those laypersons who can sing in choirs or teach or maintain property or give money, few indeed are the congregations that have taken the time to determine the secular occupations of their members. And so, when we wrote to bishops and pastors for the names of people in business management, we got few responses. Over the years, however, I have been able to identify about 450 members of the Lutheran Church in America who are in top management positions in business. It was from this group that I selected persons for my survey.

As I reviewed my mailing list, I selected 300 business leaders to whom I mailed the survey. In the letter of transmittal, I explained that I was doing a book on *In Search of Faithfulness* and asked them to be a part of my research effort. The survey itself contained fifty questions. Questions were worded in such a way that the respondents simply had to check a response block which most closely represented their view. It was not required that they sign their names, although about one-third of them did. Space was provided for any comments related to the survey and about one-fourth of the respondents provided additional thought through this means. Of the 300 survey forms which went out, 174 came back in time to be tabulated. People who do surveys will recognize that this response is unusually high. Comments volunteered by some of the respondents indicated a great interest in what I was doing.

The group is not representative of American society. Rather, it is drawn from a fairly narrow segment of our population. They are business leaders who are active members of congregations of the Lutheran Church in America. They are 93.5% male and 6.5% female. Thirty-four percent were under age fifty; 55% were between age fifty and sixty-five, while 12% were over sixty-five.

Ninety-two percent of the survey group considered themselves to be active members of their congregations, with 91.8% claiming they attend church regularly. Compare this high indication of regular church participation with the 1984 Gallup report, which showed that 39% of Protestants are in church on any given Sunday, and it can be seen that the survey group is well above average in their church attendance.

In its Northstar Poll of 712 adults done by the *St. Paul Pioneer Press and Dispatch*, WCCO Television, and WCCO Radio, it was determined that 47% of the Lutherans interviewed attended church regularly.[1] The business executives surveyed for this book, therefore, are not typical of other Lutherans in this respect. The Northstar Poll indicated that 58% of Lutherans interviewed pray daily and 27% read the Bible at least once a week. In comparison, respondents to the survey for this book indicated that 55% pray daily and 26% read the Bible "regularly."

In summary, data from my survey was drawn from top business executives who are well above average in their religious practices within Lutheran congregations.

The survey dealt with five general areas of inquiry. The series of questions in section 1 probed how the respondents looked at their faith. It is in this area that one is able to indicate an "acknowledgment" of a faith relationship with God, which is an essential part of our definition of faithfulness. Section 2 dealt with the factors that are important in shaping the ethical decision making of the business executive. Section 3 contained questions designed to reveal the factors in one's life that were important in shaping religious conviction. Section 4 investigated the degree to which respondents practiced certain religious and spiritual disciplines. Section 5 asked business people to whom they would turn when they needed to discuss a troubling problem in their occupations.

Before mailing the survey to the three hundred potential respondents, I asked about twenty business friends to test the document for me. On the basis of their suggestions, some questions were changed or reworded. Even so, a few of the respondents complained about the use of such nondefined terms as "faithfulness" and "success."

After the initial responses were put in the computer and tabulated, I worked with a professional in the field of research surveys to do the cross-tabulation necessary to identify the attributes or practices of faithfulness. Under his guidance, I have taken great care not to draw conclusions from the survey, based on too small a sample of any particular response. No percentage responses will be reported which have a margin of error greater than 5%.

In order to give a fuller picture of the nature of the group surveyed, some responses to background questions might be helpful here. Of nine key factors which were most important in shaping the religious convictions of the survey group, "formal religious teaching as a child" came out on top. This factor was rated very important by 47.7% of the replies and another 40.2% rated it important. In second place was the somewhat allied factor, "religious convictions of the family in which you were raised." Here 37.2% rated the factor as very important and an additional 46.5% rated it important.

Next in order of importance came "membership in a church," "influence of a friend or spouse," "reading the Bible," "influence of a religious leader," "reading religious books," "religious studies in school or college," and "television." However, the "influence of a friend or spouse," "reading of the Bible," and "influence of a religious leader" were so closely rated that they should be considered approximately equal in importance. That the survey group does not resonate with religious television broadcasts is obvious. Not one person in the 174 listed "television" as a very important factor in shaping their religious convictions and only 7 gave it any importance at all.

There does appear to be an element of the works-righteous theology among the survey group—24.4% of them agreed or strongly agreed with the statement "I believe God rewards his faithful people with success"; 58.3% of the respondents disagreed with the statement. There were, however, another 17.3% who registered no opinion on the statement. Since this question drew the second highest percentage of no-opinion responses of all the questions, there appears to be a lack of conviction in the doctrine of justification by faith through grace alone. However, 58.3% of the respondents disagreed with the statement. But caution is needed before being too certain of a conclusion since people define success in different ways. Nevertheless, the fact that only 58% of such strong churchgoers reject the premise that God "rewards" persons under *any* circumstances should cause pastors and church leaders some concern.

The question that drew the largest positive response of all fifty was

"I want my children and grandchildren to have a solid religious faith"; 98.8% of the business executives agreed with that statement. When asked if they themselves had a form of family worship, however, only 22.2% indicated regularly and another 36.8% indicated occasionally. Lay this alongside the fact that, as mentioned earlier, the group attributed great importance to the influence of their own family in shaping their religious convictions and one has to ask, By what means do the executives expect their children to develop a "solid religious faith"?

So much for general information about the survey. As will be seen in later chapters, the cross-tabulation of responses will be a valuable source of information as we search for the attributes of faithfulness.

THE INTERVIEWS

Along with the survey of 174 Lutheran business executives, I conducted about 70 personal interviews with people from all walks of life and from a variety of church associations. The mix was about equally distributed between male and female. The age range ran from about thirty to seventy with the heaviest representation being in the forty-five to sixty-five range.

I tried not to make the interviews too structured since I was more interested in seeing where people went with our conversation than I was in making certain every interview covered precisely the same questions. There were three general areas I sought to cover in each interview, however. First, I asked for the person's definition of faithfulness and, in some cases, success. As we discussed these terms, I occasionally found it necessary to steer the person's thinking to defining faithfulness and success as they relate to Christian living. However, I carefully avoided providing any other feedback to the person so as not to influence or shape the definitions.

Next, I asked the respondent to "describe to me some of the persons in your experience who would meet the definition of faithfulness as you have just stated it." Very little encouragement was needed here. Every person I interviewed had stories of at least two persons who stood out in their lives as faithful persons. In the vast majority of cases, the examples of faithfulness were persons well known to the respondent. In a few cases, a public person, living or dead, was cited as an example.

Finally, I asked, "Are there any attributes, values, or practices which were common among those faithful persons you just de-scribed?" In every instance the person being interviewed was able to list several. In addition, in my note taking for the second question I listed some attributes, values, and practices which were mentioned to me and which sometimes were overlooked by the respondent in his or her answer to the third question.

The selection of persons to be interviewed was largely random. Over a period of a year, as I sat talking to persons on a one-to-one basis, I would ask their help in the research work I was doing. In four instances, I met with a group and sought their help. In those cases, I asked them to write answers to the three questions on a sheet of paper. Once that was done, I asked for the response of each individual, which I noted, and then opened up the discussion among the group. These four group sessions provided the opportunity to gain insights as people discussed the subject among themselves and, at times, modified their initial written responses. In a few instances, I did seek out specific persons for an interview. My choice was based on personal knowledge I had of some unusual event or act in that person's life which, I suspected, had some direct faith implications. About fifteen of the seventy interviews were of this nature.

Obviously, reports of the interviews will be largely anecdotal. I have made no effort to do any kind of a statistical analysis of responses to my questions. I carefully collected the so-called attributes offered by interviewees and gathered them into general categories. But I have not endeavored to determine which attributes were most frequently observed by those interviewed.

CONCLUSIONS

As explained in the last chapter, the interviews contributed to the definitions established in this book for faithfulness and successfulness.

Information gained from the interviews and the survey has enabled me to suggest that there are, indeed, observable attributes of the faithful. I have identified seven. They are: (1) having a sense of identity, (2) growth, (3) prayer/meditation, (4) life in community, (5) giving, (6) sense of justice, and (7) simplicity of life style. While not every person who was cited as a model of faithfulness had all seven attributes, they almost invariably had most of them, albeit in varying degrees.

It is important to emphasize the word "degree." The Christian faith is not a static thing; it is dynamic, ever-growing. Movement has always been symbolic of the Christian perspective. We are the people of "the Way." We are growing, becoming. There is a quotation I have cherished for many years which goes, "This life, therefore, is not righteousness, but *growth* in righteousness, not health, but *healing*, not being, but *becoming*, not rest, but *exercise*. We are not yet what we shall be, but we are *growing toward it*. The process is not yet finished, but *it is going on*. This is not the end, but *it is the road*. All does not gleam in glory, but all *is being purified*." I do not know the source of that quotation, but it certainly applies to the "becoming" nature of Christian faithfulness. Joseph Sittler, in his book *Gravity and Grace*, says, "We live by faith, and it's never a finished faith."[2]

We are at different points in our growth and it would be an absolute contradiction of Christian doctrine to judge one person more worthy than another by virtue of their more mature faithfulness. The working definition of faithfulness for this book is "acknowledging God's graceful relationship with us by striving to grow more Christlike in our daily lives." Our "growth" in the faith is in response to the gift of God's unqualified relationship with us, not as a means to merit that relationship.

Therefore, as we discuss the seven attributes of faithfulness in the chapters to follow, let no one conclude that the collecting and development of them all is the means to eternal life, nor that the absence of them all is the sure and certain proof that one is beyond salvation. Judgment belongs to God, not us. We simply share with you the observations and practices of those Christians who have acknowledged God's graceful relationship with them and who are responding to that gift by striving to grow more Christlike in their daily lives.

F O U R

A SENSE OF
IDENTITY

I firmly believe that any organization, in order to survive and achieve success, must have a sound set of beliefs on which it premises all its policies and actions. Next, I believe that the most important single factor in corporate success is faithful adherence to those beliefs. And, finally, I believe if an organization is to meet the challenge of a changing world, it must be prepared to change everything about itself except those beliefs."[1] These are the words of Thomas Watson, Jr., the highly respected chief executive officer of IBM, which is itself one of the most highly respected corporations in the world. IBM, or "Big Blue" as it is affectionately called, has been touted by business analysts, business-school professors, and organizational experts as perhaps the best model of the ideal American corporation. Trace its stock market record. Talk to its employees. Listen to its competitors. All the evidence is there: it is a highly successful organization.

To what does Big Blue owe its success? "A sound set of beliefs," says its leader, to which it adheres no matter how its environment changes.

There is no doubt that successful Christian living is founded on essentially the same precept. The survey and the interviews we conducted all agreed: faithfulness begins with a "belief in" the faithfulness of God. Christians believe that they are called into a loving relationship with God which is not dependent upon their worthiness. It is a gift. It is the "acknowledgment" of that gift, to use Barth's term, which causes us to pattern our lives after that perfect model of love, Jesus Christ. It is the "faithful adherence to those beliefs," to steal the words of Tom Watson, which becomes the most important single factor in faithful (or successful) Christian living.

This faithful adherence was mentioned in many of the interviews. Will Boyer talked about the faith of his father. Will's recollections of childhood were of an invalid father, in constant pain, struggling to support a family in the grinding depths of the Great Depression. Yet, this man, with an unswerving faith in his relationship with God, was always cheerful, always optimistic, and always prepared to share with others the faith conviction he held.

So, too, with Dave Fishburn's sister. She has gone through all kinds of personal sickness and illness within her family. Dave marvels, "Yet, with all that trouble, she has a faith like the Rock of Gibraltar."

Don Breter's brother has been confined to a wheelchair for most of his life. Don spoke with passion of his brother's love for life and his tenacity. "He can go anywhere I can and can do anything I can," says Don with deep admiration. "He is a specialist in adversity," chuckles Don, "for he is constantly teaching other disabled persons about how God's faithful people in the Bible were able to live with adversity." The brother is active in his church and the strength of his convictions about God has been a source of inspiration to other members.

Numerous were the stories of beliefs being demonstrated through acts of courage and during times of adversity. There were many other stories about faithful people. John's friend quit his job because of an injustice on the part of management. Gloria's father spent all his free time visiting sick people. Another John gave up a highly respected position in medical research to take a much-lower-paying job in a center-city emergency room. Ken's friend uses his money and influence in his hometown to improve the condition of street people. Barbara regularly visits people in prison. In relating these and other tales of sacrifice and service, the people being interviewed were "certain" that the acts were the result of the acknowledgment of God's faithfulness. These people knew they had purpose in life, a mission, if you will, because of their strong belief in God's faithfulness. It was interesting to note, however, that those who were personally suffering the most were most willing to tell others of their faith convictions. Most faithful Christians go about their lives serving God by serving their brothers and sisters without articulating their faith.

Which leads to the oft-posed question, Should Christians tell others *why* they serve? Recognizing that good works are by no means done only by the faithful, does it matter that most of us do not share our beliefs with others? Whatever one's response to that question may be, it is apparent that it is in times of deepest adversity that we feel freest to tell others of our beliefs.

Tom Watson points out that the set of beliefs is the base on which an organization "premises all its policies and actions." Mission statements flow from beliefs. Function and structure flow from mission statements. Purpose and identity are articulated. But, maintains Watson, it all starts with beliefs.

Exactly so for the faithful Christian. Our mission in life, our purpose for being flows from our faith conviction. It is the foundation of our identity.

Two questions in the survey of business persons have turned out to be important. I had not anticipated how important they would be when the survey was designed, but they do stand out. One proposition reads like this: "I can feel a sense of ministry in my present job." Space is provided for the respondent to check off "strongly agree," "agree," "no opinion," "disagree," or "strongly disagree." Another statement reads, "I feel called by God to my present occupation." Again, the respondent can place a check in one of the five response columns.

Those two questions were originally introduced into the survey because they seemed to be ones which would give some clue to how persons relate faith to life, especially in their present occupations. As I began to run cross-tabulations on numerous responses to various questions, however, it began to dawn on me that those questions really deal with identity. They call upon persons to state who they see themselves to be—"I see myself as a person in ministry in my job, or I do not," "I feel called by God in my job, or I do not." In a real sense those two questions were asking persons to articulate their basic beliefs.

MINISTRY AND CALLING

What kind of results did we get? On the question asking about feeling a "sense" of ministry in one's occupation, 21.4% of the people said they strongly agreed, while another 46.2% said they agreed. That is a total positive response of 67.6%. On the other hand, 14.5% said they disagreed with that statement and only 1.7% said they strongly disagreed. The no-opinion column was marked by 16.2%, which was the third highest no-opinion response we received.

How does one view those results? On the one hand, it is nice to see that about 2/3 of the business people surveyed feel a sense of ministry in their jobs, while only 1/6 do not. That gives one some comfort that, one way or another, these people are trying to use the model of Jesus' ministry on their jobs. On the other hand, when one considers that the group surveyed were all very active churchgoers (91.8% claim to attend Sunday worship regularly), and that a fundamental teaching of the church is that our faith response is to be "little Christs" to one another, it is not too encouraging to find that about one-third of these loyal churchgoers are unable to say whether or not they "sense" a ministry in their work.

The statement about being "called by God to my present occupation" is a more audacious one. Even though we speak of the Christian's calling, we generally reserve the term for ordained clergy and those who have entered full-time church occupations. In response to this question, 6.5% of the people strongly agreed, with another 24.1% agreeing. On the other hand, 28.8% did not agree, and an additional 5.3% strongly disagreed. A surprising 35.3% registered no opinion, by far the highest no-opinion response in the entire survey.

How does one interpret these results? Again, it is quite a surprise that 30.6% of the people feel bold enough to claim that they have been called by God in their present occupation. Considering how closely identified the word "call" is to church occupations, it has to say something about how these people see their identity. And it may be some consolation that only 34.1% of the people are not able to claim a calling in their occupation. But what about the 35.3% who had no opinion? Could it be that they were too humble to claim a calling in their occupation? Could it be that they were afraid to deny the possibility of God's call in their job? Or could it be that dualism is at work, and the message from their church has never suggested that, indeed, laypersons get calls for service in the world? In short, did the question raise an issue which has never before been presented to them?

Interesting as these responses were, they became exceedingly valuable when one began running cross-tabulations. An example of one such cross-tabulation: One of the statements in the survey reads, "Persons with a solid religious faith generally are more joyful in their working lives." Of the total group 12.8% strongly agreed with this statement and an additional 65.1% agreed. On the other side, 8.1%

disagreed and only one person strongly disagreed. No opinion accounted for 13.4%.

Do people who sense a ministry in their occupations see it different from those who do not? The cross-tabulation indicates that they do. Of those people who strongly agreed that they felt a sense of ministry in their jobs, 22.2% strongly agreed that people with a solid religious faith are generally more joyful in their working lives, and another 66.7% agreed with the statement. Similarly, those who agreed on the ministry question, strongly agreed by 16.7% on the joyful question, with an additional 78.8% agreeing. The reverse was also true. Those who disagreed on the sense of ministry question also were stronger in their disagreement on the joyful question.

The same cross-tabulation between the question on calling and being joyful in their work demonstrated that those who felt they were called by God in their occupations had a much stronger conviction about joyfulness in work than those who did not feel called.

While this illustration of the cross-tabulation may not yield any surprises, it does demonstrate that positive responses to the question on ministry and calling yield significantly more positive responses to other questions than do negative responses to ministry and calling. I could find no other questions in the survey where the same pattern was universally true with respect to other questions.

In short, I am asserting that those persons who answered positively to the questions of ministry and calling have made a clearer acknowledgment of their faithful relationship with God than the rest of the group and that, therefore, their responses to other questions will weigh heavily in identifying other attributes of faithfulness.

This is not to make a judgment that, unless one can positively agree upon ministry and calling in one's occupation, one is outside a faithful relationship with God. It is God who initiates the relationship, and it is God who is faithful. What we *are* saying is that as we seek to discover the attributes of God's faithful persons, we need to pay special attention to those who have acknowledged that relationship by claiming a certain identity, a purpose, or a mission. We are never finished with growth in our faith; therefore, we can learn about growth from those who have matured in their faithfulness. It is clear that at some point in our journey of faith, we must be able to affirm a sound set of beliefs on which we premise all our actions.

In *A Search for Excellence,* Peters and Waterman arrived at a list of attributes for successful corporations as a result of intensive research, interviewing, and surveys. We have followed essentially the same procedure in our search for faithfulness. In our search for the attributes of faithfulness, however, we will turn to another, and very important, source—the life of Jesus. If we respond to God's faithful relationship with us by trying to pattern our lives in the image of Jesus, then an attribute of faithfulness is valid only if it can be seen as an attribute of his life.

THE IDENTITY OF JESUS

Well, how about it? Did Jesus have a "sound set of beliefs"? Did he acknowledge his relationship with God? Did he have a mission, a purpose for living? The answer to all these questions is clearly yes, and it seems almost unnecessary to prove it. Nevertheless, we do need to remind ourselves of several scriptural accounts. In the Gospel according to John, Jesus uses a variety of expressions to tell who he is and what was his purpose. "I am the bread of life; he who comes to me shall not hunger, and he who believes in me shall never thirst" (John 6:35). "I am the way, and the truth, and the life; no one comes to the Father, but by me" (John 14:6). "I am the good shepherd" (John 10:14).

In the Gospel according to Luke, there is clear account of Jesus' acknowledgment of his calling. It happened after the forty days of trials in the wilderness. Luke tells us he returned to Galilee, "in the power of the spirit." According to the account, Jesus went into the synagogue on the Sabbath, "as was his custom," and he stood up to read. He was given the scroll of the prophet Isaiah, and he found the place where it read, "The Spirit of the Lord is upon me, because he has anointed me to preach good news to the poor. He has sent me to proclaim release to the captives and recovering of sight to the blind, to set at liberty those who are oppressed, to proclaim the acceptable year of the Lord" (Luke 4:18–19). He rolled up the scroll, gave it back to the attendant and sat down. The eyes of everyone in the synagogue were focused on him. Then he gave them the shocker: "Today this scripture has been fulfilled in your hearing" (v.21).

An important point in the section of Isaiah which Jesus chose to read is that the actions of preaching the good news, proclaiming freedom for the prisoners, and all the rest were *as a result* of the

Lord's anointing. The anointing came from the Lord. Jesus acknowledged that gift, and responded to the call with a lifetime of teaching,
serving, and sacrifice.

We, too, have been anointed—at the time of our baptism. While
we are still babies, with no merit of our own, God names us as
one of God's people and calls us into a faithful relationship with
God. The importance of that baptismal event cannot be ignored. It
is our point of call. In fact, Luther was so bold as to say that if you
have been baptized, you have been ordained as a priest of God. And
that calling is not just for a narrow slice of our lives. We are not
called just to serve on church committees or pass collection plates
or mow the lawn at the parsonage. We are called to be the people
of God in all of our life—in our families, in our communities, in our
churches and, yes, even in our occupations. That 35% of active
churchgoing business persons have no opinion as to whether they
have been called by God in their occupations really is a disgrace and
the organized church has reason to be ashamed of it.

THE IMPORTANCE OF CALL

For years, I have been encouraging laypersons to realize that all
of us have been called by God, but the results of the survey have
made it more clear to me than ever before that the sense of call is
absolutely crucial for the faithful. As will be seen throughout the
rest of this book, those who feel they have been called respond much
more positively to other aspects of their faith than those who do not
or those who have no opinion.

About a year ago, I received a phone call from a young ordained
minister with whom I had done conference work on the ministry of
the laity some years before. He told me he had just accepted a call
as associate minister to one of the largest and most prestigious
congregations in his denomination. He saw tremendous potential
within this congregation for affirming the ministry of the laity. Many
of the parishioners, he pointed out, were in positions of power and
influence in the city. He asked if I would agree to lead a weekend
retreat on the ministry of the laity as a launching pad for his
development of this emphasis within the congregation. I agreed to
do so and we set a date some six months down the road.

About two months before the scheduled retreat, I received a phone call from the senior rector who wanted to "discuss details" of the retreat. I sensed that another purpose was behind his call, and so there was. As we talked, he said that he had read my first book, *Christianity and Real Life*, and was somewhat concerned about my present position. "Tell me," he asked in a lovely Scottish accent, "have your views changed since you wrote that book?" I said that while today I might express my feelings differently, my basic conviction about the call of all God's people into ministry remains unchanged. "Well, Mr. Diehl," he said, "that concerns me. While I agree in principle with what you say, it is a very radical idea and I'm not sure our people are ready for that as yet." Inside I cried, "What in God's name are you preaching to those people?" but, of course, I did not say it. I politely suggested that perhaps we should postpone the retreat for a year or so and when he though his people would be ready, he should give me a call. He thought that was a splendid suggestion and said he would get back to me sometime. I have not heard from him.

And so, in one of our major cities there is a large congregation, with a membership of highly influential Christians, who will safely be protected from the "radical" idea that God has called them into ministry in their daily lives. Is it any wonder the business-excellence books make no reference to religious influences in the lives of successful business executives?

We have got to get over this nonsense that the call to the ordained ministry is a "higher" call than the call to laypersons. There is *one* call—the call to all God's people—and, therefore, there is but one vocation: to be the people of God. With all due respect to my own bishop, whom I greatly admire, and with all due respect to all those wonderful, dedicated pastors whose lives I admire, I must protest the use of their reference to a "special call" to the ordained ministry, because that word "special" is meant to mean "higher."

I do not understand why the clergy are so uptight about the generous use of the terms "ministry" and "call." Ministry is not a zero-sum game. To have laity in ministry does not lessen the ministry of the ordained; it *multiplies* it. To affirm the call of laypersons is not to diminish the call of the ordained.

When one answers one's call by going into the ordained ministry, one indeed does assume a particular responsibility and a particular function. As Joseph Sittler put it, "The ordained ones are the tellers of that story without which the church was not, is not, and cannot continue. But, cannot others tell the story? The church must keep its story going and assure that there will never be a time or place where the sacraments, commanded by Christ, are not proffered. Therefore, the church insists on preparing a designated cadre to see to it that the constitutive story is told, and that the nurturing sacraments are administered. This is a way of defining ordained ministers that does not elevate it above the laity, but gives it a particular job among the people of God."[2]

I affirm that position fully. I also affirm that a mother has a particular job among the people of God. So does a teacher, a doctor, a business person, a carpenter, a farmer. And the churches better get with it in affirming these people's particular ministries as their calling.

Every time I have discussed the subject of ministry of the laity in depth with a group of clergy, there comes a point at which someone will use the term "anticlerical." That is the signal that I have gone too far, and it has always caused me to try to do a better job of "explaining" what I mean. I try to soothe ruffled feathers. No layperson, who is trying to work within the church, can get tarred with the charge of being "anticlerical" and survive. So, we are very careful not to be too strident. We tiptoe around so as not to offend.

But has anyone considered that pastors who refuse to recognize the calling or ministry of their lay people are, in fact, anti-lay? The results of these surveys demonstrated, very powerfully, the importance of a sense of identity—a knowledge of calling—in determining faithfulness. When only 30% of active churchgoing, business persons can say that they feel they have been called by God in their occupations, something is wrong, and our ordained ministers, the "tellers of the story," must largely be held accountable for the scandal.

FIVE

GROWTH

Some of the writing for this book was done during our annual vacation at the shore. For sixteen years, we have been going to Bethany Beach, Delaware, staying at the same house on the beach. My morning routine is usually the same: rise early, a period of quiet time, a jog on the beach, and then off to the store for the morning papers. This year, as I made my first appearance in the familiar store and had selected the usual newspapers, the elderly woman behind the counter said, "$1.45 for the B.C." "The what?" "The B.C." "What's the B.C.?" I asked, somewhat amused. "It's the Business-man's Combination," she said. "You got 'em right there: the *New York Times*, the *Wall Street Journal*, and the *Washington Post*. It's what all the businessmen get. It's the B.C. and it costs $1.45." Incredible! I thought. Are we that much alike?

And so for the rest of the week, I just walked up to the counter with my armload of newspapers, said, "B.C.," and plunked down my money. Saved a lot of time. The old woman did not have to check out what I had. She knew.

The *Wall Street Journal* sells more copies each day than any other newspaper in America—1.99 million copies daily. In any conversation of business persons, and I mean *any*, you quote an article or essay from the *Journal* and you know that the majority of the people present have read that same article. You may be excused for having missed a particular issue of the *Journal* because of some unusual circumstances, but a business person never, never, says he or she does not read that newspaper. It is the bible of American business. In fact, a number of years ago Dr. Carnegie Calian wrote a book called *The Gospel According to The Wall Street Journal*[1] in which he compared the *Journal's* gospel with the Christian gospel. There were differences.

As one travels around the country, the companion paper to the *Journal* is the *New York Times,* the *Washington Post,* the *Chicago Times,* or the *Los Angeles Times,* depending on where you are. Sorry, folks, do not quote the *Boston Globe* or the *Philadelphia Inquirer* or the *Fort Worth Star Telegram,* or the *San Francisco Examiner.* They are not in the same league as far as business people are concerned.

All of this is simply to point out that business people regularly, and I mean regularly, read those newspapers which have been established as the ones which must be read if one is to function in the business world. It is an absolute necessity if one is to grow in the world of business.

And, what about the world of religion? Do business persons just as avidly read their Bibles as they do their *Journals?* Is a good knowledge of scriptures considered a requirement for growth in one's life?

It has been my experience that business people are, as a group, biblical illiterates. One of the most embarrassing experiences I undergo is to listen to a business person try to make a point on any issue by referring to the Bible. They usually either misquote or misunderstand the scriptural reference they cite. Of course, there are exceptions, but I fear that for the majority their only acquaintance with the Bible occurs on a Sunday morning when the lessons are read in the worship service.

I am not alone in that assessment. Richard R. Gilbert, in the foreword to *Business, Religion and Ethics,* reports on a conference held at Princeton Theological Seminary in which business leaders from the Fortune 500 joined with pastors and theologians to deal with the relationship of ethics and religion to business. "One thing stood out boldly," writes Gilbert. "Business leaders were largely innocent of biblical ethics."[2]

Our survey of business persons tended to bear out the harsh criticisms of biblical ignorance. Of the group, 25.9% indicated that they read the Bible regularly. The term "regularly" was not defined for them. Another 42.9% said they read it occasionally; 31.2% seldom or never read the Bible.

The survey results were not much different from the Northstar Poll conducted by the *St. Paul Pioneer Press and Dispatch* and published in its June 9, 1985, edition. In this random telephone survey of 712 adults, 24% claimed to read the Bible weekly, 10% said monthly, 44% said occasionally, and 22% said never.

Although the results of both polls correlate somewhat, there is a significant point to observe. The Northstar Poll was conducted among *all* citizens, not just churchgoers, while our poll was conducted among a group in which 92.4% claimed to be active members of their churches. In short, business persons who claim to be active members of their congregations read their Bibles with the same infrequency as does the general public. No one needs to take a poll of those same business people to conclude that they read the *Wall Street Journal* with far greater frequency than does the general public.

On the other hand, when we look at those business respondents who strongly agreed that they felt a sense of ministry in their jobs, 50% claimed to be regular readers of the Bible. For those who strongly felt called by God in their present occupations, 72.7% read the Bible with regularity. That is a striking difference.

If a part of the definition of faithfulness involves the growth of striving to become more Christlike in one's daily life, then we need to search for evidence that Jesus was biblically literate. It is an easy search. In the Gospel according to Matthew, Jesus quotes scriptures on twenty-eight separate occasions and acts so as to "fulfill scripture" on nine additional occasions. In Mark he quotes the Old Testament seventeen times and twice he acts to fulfill scriptures. In Luke the numbers are nineteen and two; in John, six and six. There is not the least doubt that Jesus was well versed in the scriptures of his day.

One might argue that, whereas the *Wall Street Journal* is a report of constantly changing news, the Bible is a fixed quantity of material. It is not changing every day, or even every year. Therefore, one might conclude that once a person has read the Bible completely, there really is no need for regular rereading.

My personal experience indicates otherwise. The fact of the matter is that *we* are constantly changing. Not only do we pass through many stages of life, but we frequently experience new and different events which have an impact on our lives. At a certain point in one's life or after a special experience, a part of scripture which was overlooked in past readings suddenly comes alive for us.

A few years ago, our denomination's publishing house came out with a new Bible study program called "Word and Witness." Although it had been several years since I had participated in an intensive Bible study program, I was somewhat uncertain about my investment of time in this one. Would thirty-nine weeks of intensive Bible study really yield new learnings, commensurate with such a massive commitment of time? It seemed hardly possible. But I gave it a try. Much to my astonishment, there was a constant stream of new learnings. It almost made me wonder if I had *ever* really studied the Bible before.

There is, of course, a difference between Bible *reading* and Bible *study*. The study programs involve the utilization of historical and theological resources to help one fully understand the context and purpose of certain sections of the Bible. On the other hand, Bible reading is simply working one's way through the scriptures as a part of one's daily meditative routine. I have found it useful to recycle the psalms in my morning meditation and work my way through the New Testament in my bedtime readings. The evening readings may be as much as a chapter or as little as a few verses. I read until I hit something that causes me to do a bit of reflecting—or until my eyes begin to close, whichever comes first. It seems to me, however, that both Bible study and Bible reading are important elements of one's faith journey.

What we are really talking about is growth. If, as human beings, we do not grow, we stagnate. We atrophy. It is true of us physically, mentally, emotionally, socially, and spiritually.

For persons in business, growth is not solely the result of regularly reading the *Wall Street Journal.* Experience is a great teacher, and who does not grow as the result of many experiences in life? During my early career, as a salesman for Bethlehem Steel, there was a conviction that experience was not only the best teacher for a young salesperson, it was the *only* teacher. "Drop 'em in the river and see if they can swim!" was the advice given by old-timers as they saw new college graduates coming into the sales organization. "Good salesmen are born, not made." That philosophy was terribly wasteful as one young salesperson after another would repeat mistakes that any skilled instructor could have helped them avert.

Today it is quite different. Most major corporations have extensive training programs for new employees, including the development of selling skills. An entire profession has grown up around the development of employees within an organization. Not only are development programs offered within most companies, but there are countless consultants and organizations offering a plethora of seminars and courses on development and growth.

I am a member of the American Management Association. The organization offers courses, seminars, books, audiotapes, videotapes, and research reports designed to help managers grow in their skills. It is without exaggeration to say that I receive at least four mailings each week from the AMA, promoting one of its services. There is a constant outpouring of conferences held sequentially in various cities in the United States. American Management Association even has its own book-publishing plant. Development and growth in the world of business is a big business in itself.

So, what do we have to offer the same business persons to assist them in their spiritual growth? Not much. At least, not much of any quality.

One of the questions we asked in our survey of business persons was to what degree they participated in adult education programs at their church. Of the total number surveyed, 26.3% said they regularly did, while an additional 42.7% said they did occasionally. But a closer look at the data shows something quite interesting.

As we are seeing throughout this book, those persons who feel very positive about being in ministry or have a feeling they have been called by God almost without exception respond to questions about their faith practices much more positively than those who do not share such impressions. But with respect to adult education in the congregation there is very little difference. For example, of those who agree that they feel they have a ministry in their jobs, 31% regularly participate in adult education programs and 46.5% do so occasionally. For those who feel they have been called by God, the responses are 29.4% and 45.1%. From a statistical standpoint, these numbers are so close to the responses of all those surveyed as to be considered almost identical.

What is going on? What is the problem? Why not a more positive response from those who have a high spiritual commitment?

The problem lies with the quality of adult education offered within our church structures. There is no question that the church is well suited to present courses on Bible study, dogmatics, church history, theology, and spirituality. It also has a degree of competence in dealing with such issues as suffering, family relationships, death and dying, interpersonal relationships, and the like. But, with very few exceptions, our churches are very weak in the "how-to" or "connections" teachings.

Americans are a people of the "how-tos." One goes into a bookstore today and finds shelf after shelf of books devoted to the "how-tos." How to lose weight. How to make a fortune in the stock market. How to fix a Volkswagon. How to grow a lovely lawn. How to play golf better. How to build a bird house. How to cook. How to improve one's SAT scores. How to travel in Europe on a low budget. On and on they go.

Yet where, in our church education programs, do we deal with the how-tos of connecting faith and life within the context of our daily activities? Taking business people as our example, what does the gospel of Jesus Christ have to do with the union movement, with protectionism, with competition, with federal regulation of business, with corporate takeovers, with plant closings, with sex discrimination? One could go on and on. And one might ask why any of these issues should be discussed with relation to the gospel. Why indeed? Simply because our God is passionately concerned about the welfare of all people and each of these topics directly affects the lives of God's children. And so, for the business person it should be a matter of utmost faith for him or her to find the connections or how-tos for relating the teachings of the church to these complex issues of the day. But, since the church does not try to make these connections, it is only natural that business persons conclude that they live in two worlds. Dualism thrives.

What has been said about business persons is equally true for all of us. Whether we work as educators, health providers, homemakers, lawyers, builders, farmers, bankers, craftspersons, social workers, or public service workers, there are problems and decisions facing us that affect the welfare of other persons. If God's faithful are to be trying to mirror the life of Jesus, then it is important that the means be provided to help them see how the life and teachings of Jesus apply to the everyday situations they face. They must be able to *experience* their faith. Too much of the religious education provided by the church deals with the *content* of belief while ignoring the *experience* of belief. Content is important but it must connect with experience.

In a report prepared for the Religious Education Association of the United States and Canada, Dr. Constance Leean studied faith development among adults. The study revealed that most people do not equate faith with a set of beliefs or dogma, but see it more experiential. Dr. Leean concludes that Christian education programs should provide for "discussions of personal faith experiences."[3] You got it, Dr. Leean!

While the local congregation is the appropriate location for the study of the Bible, church history, theology, and the like, it may not be the best place for relating theology and the Bible to complex issues facing people in the workplace. The reason is that the pastor, who has been trained in theology and biblical studies, cannot be expected to have an adequate enough understanding of the complexities of workplace problems to do a credible job of pointing to the how-tos of connecting faith and life. A common complaint among business persons is that the clergy do not understand economics and, as a consequence, make simplistic statements and draw erroneous conclusions when speaking on that subject. In all fairness to the pastors, it must be conceded that the business people do *not* complain when the pastors say nice things about them, even though such statements may be simplistic or erroneous. Nevertheless, it is true, pastors are not experts in business or medicine or law or world affairs. Nor should they be expected to be so.

Somewhat the same situation applies to seminaries of the church. In recent years many of them have set out to provide adult education programs for laypersons. The motive for doing so is to increase income for the financially strapped institutions, but that is beside the point. The point is that the courses offered are primarily adaptations of what are offered to the theological students themselves. Several of my friends who administer continuing education programs at various seminaries are frustrated that their lay programs do not attract more people. Yet, the reason should be obvious: They are not touching the experiences of the persons they are trying to attract.

Because the congregation's professional staff cannot possibly be the resource experts on many societal issues, other channels for stimulating discussions of personal faith experiences need to be available, such as academies, conferences, and retreats.

One movement that has met with success over the past forty years in stimulating adult Christian education and growth is the Evangelical Academy movement of Western Europe.

This movement, which appears to be strongest in West Germany, got its start shortly after the end of World War II. Germany was in virtual disarray, and the horrors of the war were coupled with the realization that the nation had been led into disastrous and barbarous ventures. How could a nation so torn and destroyed begin the process of rebuilding?

The Evangelical Academy movement, born in 1945 at Bad Boll, was the church's contribution to the rebuilding of a decent society. Since that time, numerous Academies have been established (twelve in Germany alone), each specializing in particular issues such as economics, public service, education, and culture and communication. As the society has changed, so too have the foci of the Academies.

While the Academies receive 70 percent of their financial support from the *Landeskirchen* or regional churches, they have a programmatic independence and have no direct connections with local parishes. The substantial financial support has enabled them to maintain full-time staff (as many as fifty-five at Bad Boll) with special expertise in certain areas.

One can appreciate the magnitude of adult education which goes on by the fact that in a typical year, 1978, Bad Boll held 423 conferences, involving 15,100 participants for 36,047 days of room and board. That is a big enterprise.

Is there a place for an Academy-type movement in the United States? There is growing evidence that the answer to that is yes. In 1984, a group of Lutheran laypersons formed a nonprofit corporation, known as The Lutheran Academy, for the sole purpose of providing events and occasions where persons from various fields of endeavor could come together to discuss and debate issues facing them in daily life, within the context of theological and biblical perspectives.

The Lutheran Academy has elected not to own real estate, as do the German Academies, but instead to offer its conferences in various parts of the United States. An early conference on "The Social Impact of Industrial Change," presented in Los Angeles, brought together business persons, sociologists, economists, and theologians to examine how the structural change in America's economy was affecting society. As a follow-up to this conference, The Lutheran Academy presented one on "Societal Change and the Family," at Madison, Wisconsin, some months later. Here, sociologists, family counselors, educators, parish pastors, and theologians examined more deeply what was happening to the American family.

Business people turned out in large numbers for a conference on "The Church and the U.S. Economy," to grapple with the content of the pastoral letter of the U.S. Roman Catholic Bishops. What was the role of the church in American economic affairs? Widely differing views were expressed by business persons and church leaders, but many reported that it was the first time they were able to engage each other on this issue in an environment of openness. The conference theologian worked hard at making the biblical and theological connections.

Other conferences have been held on "Television and the Family," "Work and Identity," "Christian Faith and Political Action," "The Global Economy: Where Faith and Economics Meet," "Prophets and Profits," and others. In each instance, the target audience is those laypersons who are directly involved in their daily work with the theme of the conference. In each instance, a skilled theologian functions as a listener and a commentator on the biblical and theological connections.

The most frequent comment from laypersons who have attended a conference of The Lutheran Academy is "this is the first time I have been to a church-related event where I have been asked to share my experience in my occupation. It's great!" The conference theologians invariably report that they return to their teaching at the seminary with a broader vision of how they need to prepare future clergy for their careers.

Should similar Academy movements develop in other denominations? Should the Academy movement become interdenominational? Because it is so obviously helping the faithful in their growth as Christians, the answer to both questions should be a resounding yes. But whether it will is uncertain. Dualism is alive and well.

RETREATS

During the interviews I conducted, there were a number of instances reported where one of the faithful had a peak learning experience during a weekend retreat. Read the words of one business executive regarding the weekend retreat which, he says, has changed his life: "My three days turned out to be a revelation—not a visit, mind you, not a weekend away from home, but an absolute, total revelation of another world of infinite and indescribable beauty . . . a world where I actually met God and God turned out to be love."

A three-day period away from home seems to be an almost certain means for growth. The concentration of attention to a particular subject or theme for a full weekend is far superior to an equal number of hours of study spread over several months. The change of scenery and the lack of distractions clear the mind for new learnings and self-discovery.

Because of my years of work on the ministry of the laity, I frequently receive calls from some distant city to come and present a sermon or teach one session of an adult class on the ministry of the laity. I no longer accept such invitations because I have discovered that a twenty-minute sermon or a one-hour class session do not change lives, at least not when I do them. But I have discovered that when about thirty persons commit to spending an entire weekend together at some retreat location to study the ministry of their own lives, things do happen. Out of a group of thirty persons, there will always be two or three who later say that their lives were changed that weekend. I have never seen it to fail.

"But, people are so busy" is the usual comment. "They can't spare the time to go away for a weekend."

Are the tasks of life we undertake more important than the ones undertaken by Jesus? Although he was always on the move in his short period of ministry, he took the time to get away for renewal and reflection. Matthew tells us that when Jesus heard of the death of John the Baptist, "He withdrew from there in a boat to a lonely place apart" (Matt. 14:13). Mark reports that when the press of things had become too heavy for him and the apostles, he said to them, "Come away by yourselves to a lonely place, and rest a while" (Mark 6:31). Luke writes that "Jesus withdrew to the wilderness and prayed" (Luke 5:16).

Busy people can find the time to do anything they wish. It is simply a matter of priorities. It is apparent from the witness of others and from my own experience that if we are to grow as Christians, there are times when we must go off to a quiet place for study or reflection.

Usually a weekend retreat will involve a planned program of study among a community of friends or strangers. Perhaps it may be a program planned by the staff of the retreat center and open to anyone who is interested. Or, it may be a program planned especially for a particular group, for a particular purpose.

For some the solitary retreat weekend is an important part of spiritual growth. To be alone in the mountains or at the shore for a few days with full time given to reading books and reflecting upon one's life is an effective means for growth for some. There are a wide range of books written by those who have traveled their own pilgrimage of faith: Saint Augustine, Brother Lawrence, Thomas à Kempis, Luther, Calvin, John Wesley, Thomas Merton, Thomas Kelly, Dietrich Bonhoeffer, C. S. Lewis, Elton Trueblood, Paul Tournier, Frederick Buechner, and many others. The range of their styles and content is very broad. They are important writers whose works, unfortunately, will seldom if ever be offered within a congregational education program. Indeed, how does one learn of the classic books of the Christian faith or the latest ones on Christian thought? Not through a congregational education program. While denominational magazines generally do carry book reviews, they are inclined to favor the products of their own publishing houses. And how many people read the monthly magazine circulated by their denomination?

Care must be taken about placing all the blame for inadequate faith development upon the church and its congregation. Each of us has a responsibility for our own growth. There is a sign which can frequently be found on the walls of the offices of corporate training people. It says, "All development is self-development." Unless one is committed to growing in the faith, no amount of suggestions from the church institution will make a bit of difference. The stories of faithful people which unfolded during the surveys generally were about those who had assumed responsibility for their own spiritual maturing.

The survey supported this observation. While only 29.4% of those who felt called by God in their jobs regularly participated in congregational adult education programs, 43.1% of them said they regularly read current religious books or magazines and an additional 47.1% said they did so occasionally. I would conclude from this data that while congregational adult education programs are not very helpful to this group of business executives, it is not cause for abandoning the quest for faith development. They have found other means for stimulating their growth.

Unfortunately, however, the principle of self-development in matters of the faith makes many church leaders nervous. After all, how can denominational orthodoxy be maintained if people are out there buying all sorts of religious books? Consequently, very little encouragement comes from the pulpit or from denominational education divisions for God's people to be using any resources other than those produced in-house. This parochialism goes so far that educational materials produced by The American Lutheran Church have been discouraged for use in congregations of the Lutheran Church in America. Never mind the issue of quality; it is orthodoxy which must be preserved.

It is clear that one of the marks of God's faithful people is that they continue to grow and develop. It is unfortunate that in so many ways their own congregations get in the way of individual faith development. Changes are needed. Adult education programs must provide for greater exchange of experiences among the people, not solely content. Much more time must be spent on the how-tos of connecting the doctrines of the faith to the experiences of daily life. People should be encouraged to take the initiative in their own faith development. If the church has done its job well in teaching its doctrine, there need be no fear about the people coming in contact with "unorthodox" Christian resource materials.

SIX

PRAYER/MEDITATION

What is the most important activity in achieving success in the eyes of American chief executive officers? Managing people? No. Delegation? No. It is communication. According to the study done for the American Management Association, CEOs feel the most important thing they must do is to communicate clearly with others. And they recognized that communication is a two-way process. "The most important lesson I've had to learn," wrote one CEO, "is how to keep my mouth shut to hear what others are trying to tell me."[1] In fact, one CEO, when asked to rate the three most important things learned during his rise to the top, listed "listening . . . listening . . . listening."[2]

For the Christian, prayer is one of the chief channels of communicating with God. It is the primary means for establishing one's contact with the Creator. Anyone who attends Sunday worship services participates in the experience of prayer. So it is a given that all the people surveyed and interviewed for this book do pray. It is impossible to imagine any person claiming to be a Christian who does not pray, at least in church. But, what about outside church? What about at home or at one's place of work? What about daily prayer?

According to the Northstar Poll referred to in chapter 3, 57% of the people claimed they prayed daily; 17% claimed to pray at least weekly, outside of church; while 5% said they did so monthly; 12% said occasionally; and 8% said never.

The survey conducted among business executives yielded somewhat similar results—55% of them said they regularly had daily personal prayer, while another 26.9% said they occasionally did; 15.8% said they seldom had personal prayer outside church, and

2.3% said never. However, when one remembers that the group of business executives had a higher level of church participation than did the people polled by the newspaper, the level of daily personal prayer among the executives was not all that great. One wonders if business executives are as attentive to communicating with their Creator as they are to communicating with their associates.

Among those business persons who have acknowledged God's graceful relationship with them, however, the level of personal prayer is much higher. For example, among those who agreed that they felt a sense of ministry in their occupation, 62.9% had regular daily prayer. Conversely, among those who did not feel a sense of ministry in their jobs, only 38.2% prayed daily. Even more striking was the response from those who have felt called by God in their occupations. Here, 76.4% reported regular daily prayer.

As I conducted the interview with people, it became clear that personal prayer outside of a church worship service was an absolute attribute of God's faithful people. While not everyone claimed that daily personal prayer was an essential mark of faithful Christians, the vast majority felt that way. And no one, but no one, felt that the faithful pray only in church.

Patterns of prayer life were very diverse among the people interviewed. The majority of people seemed to have developed a routine for daily prayers. John says he has a short personal prayer every morning on the commuter train going to work. He added that, due to this routine, he frequently overlooks prayer on Saturdays. Margaret had a similar pattern of praying while she drives to work. But she confessed that traffic was very distracting and occasionally she would angrily react to another driver in the midst of prayer.

Prayer at mealtime also varied greatly. Most commonly, if the family is gathered for an evening meal and young children are present, grace is offered. Sometimes the parent prays; sometimes the child is asked to do so. In some cases, the family jointly recites a familiar prayer. Family prayer is less common at breakfast. Several families included either a Bible reading or a daily meditation reading prior to offering prayer at evening mealtime. It was considered to be an important part of their children's Christian development. More common, however, were personalized family worship programs at special feast days such as Thanksgiving, Christmas, Easter, and the birthday of a family member.

It was interesting to note that if husband and wife are sharing the meal without the children present, prayer is frequently omitted. And few, indeed, are those who pray before meals in public restaurants. A large share of the people interviewed indicated that they had some type of prayer before retiring in the evening. Evening prayer seemed to be more prevalent than morning prayer. The common pattern of evening prayer was that it was individual, silent, and personal. A number of persons indicated that they prayed the Lord's Prayer and then some personal prayer before sleep. Many acknowledged that the practice was one begun as a child. At the risk of being judgmental, it appeared to me that prayer patterns related more to children and childhood than to adulthood. That is, many adults are continuing the prayers and times of prayer that they learned as children and they seem to be more intentional about prayer when they have children of their own. It is risky to draw such conclusions from the nondirected interviews I conducted, but the suspicion is there.

As one reads the Gospel accounts of Jesus' prayer life, it appears that his times of prayer were more intense than the practices of most of us today. There are indications that Jesus frequently went off to a quiet place to spend extended time in prayer. Luke tells us, "In those days [Jesus] went out to the mountain to pray; and all night he continued in prayer to God" (6:12). It appears that he had a regular discipline of prayer. Luke tells us (22:39) that Jesus went out "as was his custom" to the Mount of Olives for prayer. He gave thanks to God prior to the distribution of food to the multitude in the miracle of the loaves and fishes.

Both Matthew and Luke tell how Jesus taught the Lord's Prayer to his disciples. But Mark's account is more detailed. Warning against hypocrites who love to pray standing in the synagogues and on the street corners in order to be seen by men, Jesus instructs that one should "go into your room and shut the door and pray to your Father who is in secret" (Matt. 6:6).

Prayer was the means by which Jesus communicated with his Father, God, and it is clear that he frequently spent extended periods of time in deep prayer. When we read accounts of the great giants of the faith, it is startling to realize how much time they, too, gave to prayer. Martin Luther said, "I have so much business I cannot get on without spending three hours daily in prayer." John Wesley is said to have spent two hours daily in prayer. Spending that much time in prayer seems to be totally out of reach and reason for most of us today. However, I was surprised to interview one man, a businessman, in fact, who spends thirty minutes in prayer each morning. He was an exception.

But with the patterns of Jesus' prayer life and with the examples of others who have walked in his footsteps, we have to ask ourselves if most of us do not have a vastly underdeveloped prayer life. Have we really grown much in prayer since we were ten years old? Is our prayer life still composed of the equivalent of asking God for a new red wagon or an "A" in the mathematics test or a smile from the pretty girl down the street? Jesus emphatically said that we are to ask God for our needs, even though God already knows of them. But is that the totality of prayer?

Remember the executive who, in the American Management Association study, said, "The most important lesson I've had to learn is how to keep my mouth shut to hear what others are trying to tell me"? Communications is a two-way process, although many of us are very poor at listening. It takes time and patience to be a good listener and most of us are much too busy to make such time available. I picked that up in the interviews conducted for this book. Most of the people referred to prayer in the sense of "talking *to* God." Very few people used the expression "talking *with* God." If listening is an important part of everyday communications in a marriage, with children, in a job, or any kind of social interchange, then should it not be an important part of prayer? But, how does one listen to God in prayer?

MANAGING TIME

In the American Management Association survey report on *How American Chief Executives Succeed,* the question was asked, "What are the three most difficult parts of your job as an executive?" The top difficulty was "planning." In second place was "time management." The two are closely related.

It seems quite obvious that a primary function of a CEO is to be involved in planning for the future of the organization. While the staff may prepare studies and suggest options and scenarios, it is the CEO who must digest all the data and come to some conclusions about the direction of the organization. So if planning is such a

common element of a CEO's job description, why do most of them
list it as their chief difficulty?

The answer is time. Time management was listed as the second
most difficult problem for CEOs. In the management consulting work
I do it is frequently listed as *the* most troublesome problem for *all*
levels of management. "How can I do my job when there are so
many telephone interruptions?" "Why must I drop everything I'm
doing to do a rush job on a report for someone who wasn't planning
ahead?" "Why does the plant manager constantly ask me questions
when he already knows the answers?" "How can I do my work
when we spend so much time in meetings?" The questions and
complaints seem endless. One salesman I know, in response to a
request from the home office for a report on why sales were down,
wrote, "The reason I can't get more business is that I'm too busy
writing reports on why I'm not getting more business!"

Interruptions and surprises go with the territory if one is in
management. But it is equally true for many occupations. Parents
have constant disruptions during the child-raising years. Secretaries
must be able to adjust to frequent interruptions in their work day.
And so, for many of us, there is the feeling that there is simply not
enough time in the day to do all the things we want to do. Time
management is a skill that few of us have successfully developed.
And for that reason, many books have been written and many
speeches have been made on how to manage one's time more
effectively.

And that is the problem for CEOs also. Because they have difficulty
in managing time, they tend to put off those things that can wait.
Crises must be dealt with immediately. Deadlines must be met. But
planning can be done "later." Many a CEO has promised to devote
time to planning, "as soon as I get all this stuff out of my way." The
problem is that new "stuff" appears and planning is forever post-
poned.

Those CEOs who are successful at planning have learned that they
must make the time available for it and hold it sacred. A good
strategy is to get away somewhere where phones and associates
cannot interrupt. There is something about a different environment
which helps clear the mind for creative thinking.

What does all this have to do with prayer? If prayer is a two-way process and requires time for listening, and if our busy days make it difficult to find time for meditation, then we need to do some time management of our own and find the occasions and places where we can listen to God.

Jesus did. Imagine, if you will, the kind of interruptions Jesus had once the word got around that he was healing the sick, giving sight to the blind, chasing out demons, and even restoring life to the dead! The Gospels are chock-full of stories of his healings. It had to be wild. How in the world could a person with so much notoriety have time for meditation? He planned for it. He made the time.

In the first chapter of Mark we get a picture of the situation. We are told that Jesus went to the home of Simon and Andrew and healed Simon's mother-in-law from a fever. The word got around town fast. Mark writes, "That evening, at sundown, they brought to him all who were sick or possessed with demons. And the whole city was gathered together about the door. And he healed many who were sick with various diseases" (1:32–34). How does someone in that kind of limelight get any personal time for meditation? Mark tells us how. He continues, "And in the morning, a great while before day, he rose and went out to a lonely place, and there he prayed" (1:35).

Matthew tells us of another time at which Jesus felt the need to get away and be alone. We are told of the occasion of the beheading of John the Baptist and how his disciples buried his body and then went to Jesus with the news. "When Jesus heard this," writes Matthew, "he withdrew from there in a boat to a lonely place apart" (14:13). However, the crowds followed him and his plans for meditation were put aside in order to heal the sick.

Luke also relates how Jesus had to make time and space for meditation. Luke reports, "Yet the news about him spread all the more, so that crowds of people came to hear him and to be healed of their sicknesses. But Jesus often withdrew to lonely places and prayed" (5:15–16 NIV).

The accounts of the Gospel writers make such frequent references to his withdrawing from the center of activity in order to pray that it has to be concluded that Jesus frequently planned periods for meditation and prayer.

In the survey of business executives, I asked to what extent they had a quiet time for meditation—26.3% of them indicated that they regularly provided for such time, and another 41.5% said they occasionally had such periods. Among those who have acknowledged their calling, however, the numbers are considerably higher. For those who feel they have been called by God in their present occupation, 47.1% regularly provide a quiet time for meditation and an additional 41.1% do it occasionally.

MEDITATION

We need to discuss what we mean by the word "meditation." I have been linking it closely with prayer, because that is the way it has been within the experience of my life. For me, meditation is prayer, but it involves both speaking and listening to God. It is the period of prayer when we are able to hear from God. Unlike Eastern forms of meditation in which one strives to become totally detached from the world, Christian meditation is the clearing of one's mind so that God's will for our involvement in the world can be sensed.

How does this happen? As I talked to people about their private meditation, it became obvious that the most common means for hearing God was through the written word. Some people interviewed used a quarterly or annual devotional book as a means of meditating. The typical format is that for every day of the year there is a Bible verse, a few paragraphs of commentary on contemporary life, and a very short prayer. However, I found that, among those who regularly provide time for meditation, such materials are inadequate. More often than not, these people are gradually working their way through a meditative book.

I asked a group of nine friends, all of whom practice daily meditation, what they were using or have recently used as a help. This is the list I received: *A Testament of Devotion* by Thomas Kelly;[3] *Celebration of Discipline* by Richard Foster;[4] *Diary of Private Prayer* by John Baillie;[5] *Meditations on a Loving God* and *Epistles Now*, both by Leslie Brandt;[6] *Now and Then* and *The Hungering Dark*, both by Frederick Buechner;[7] *With Open Heart* by Michael Quoist;[8] and *Creative Broodings* by Robert Raines.[9] The last one was a recycling of an old-timer.

One of the members of the group, the only pastor among us, startled me by saying he was reading *The Hardy Executive: Health*

Under Stress[10] during his meditation periods. At first I was surprised about his choice but, as we talked about the purpose of meditation, his selection made a good deal of sense. As a pastor in a congregation where unemployment and economic uncertainty was running high, he felt the need to read a book that related to his current situation, while all the time asking the question, "What is God's will for me in this situation?"

All of the group also said that Bible reading was a part of their period of meditation. In the last chapter we discussed Bible study. There is a difference between Bible reading and Bible study. In Bible study one learns about the context in which sections of the Bible were written, about the author and purpose of a particular book of the Bible, and about the nuances of meanings of words. In Bible reading one considers the words on the page within the context of one's own life. "What do these words have to do with me at this point in my life?" is an appropriate question to ask oneself during Bible reading.

I do not feel there is a "right way" for meditation, but in an effort to give one example of how it can be approached, here is a pattern which has been meaningful for me. I have two periods of meditation each day: one is disciplined and structured, the other is less so. Every morning I allocate about twenty minutes for meditation. That means the alarm clock must be set accordingly, depending upon what my schedule is for that day. The meditation is absolutely first on the day's agenda. I do not turn on the news or eat breakfast or shower first. Meditation is first. I usually go downstairs to a favorite chair and first read from whatever book I am working my way through. At the present time, I am reading, for the third time around, Brandt's *Epistles—Now*. I will read one section (about one and one-half pages) each day. Putting the book down, I pause to reflect on how the words that I have just read relate to the events of my day. Sometimes there are startling connections; sometimes there is nothing. Then I read one of the psalms. I continually recycle the 150 psalms, which means that I go through them about two and one-half times each year. Again, I pause to think of what those words might be saying to me personally. I then turn to the Lutheran Book of Worship and read, at random, one of the hymns. Again, there are times when the words have particular significance for me.

Then I turn to prayer. I begin by giving thanks, and that is easy for all of us, for there is so much for which we can be thankful. Then comes a period of personal intercessory prayer for Judy, my wife, and all our children and grandchildren. Next comes intercessory prayer for my mother, who is old and in a nursing home, and for other family and friends in special need. My last part of intercessory prayer is for those afflicted by particular tragedy or in special need: victims of a terrorist, people starving in Africa, those left homeless by an earthquake, or whatever similar needs have been brought to my attention.

Finally, I turn to my agenda for the day. I will go down the list of things scheduled for the day: a meeting with a client in the morning, a United Way board meeting at noon, a difficult report to write in the afternoon, a visit from one of our children for dinner, an evening with friends. For each of these scheduled events, I pray that I may be open to the possibilities of carrying out ministry with and to those with whom I will come in contact. My closing petition is that my own ego and selfish desires will be pushed aside to make way for the will of God and the presence of Jesus.

My morning meditation usually takes about twenty minutes or more, depending upon how my mind is directed. Sometimes I finish in fifteen minutes and know immediately that I was pushing myself so as to get on to other things. In a way, the clock keeps me honest.

In the evening, prior to sleep, Judy and I always pray the Lord's Prayer together. We have done so for the thirty-eight years we have been married. Sometimes it is perfunctory; sometimes it is very meaningful for us. Then we each have our own period of meditation. I read a section from the New Testament, recycling it at whatever speed it seems to go. I read until I hit something that causes me to think about it. Sometimes it will take more than a chapter to hit a point of reflection; sometimes just a few verses will bring it about. Then I turn to some other reading—any kind of reading. The bookcase, which is part of the headboard, has a wide variety of partly read books in it. There are books on economics, management, religion, philosophy, science, and the like. Whatever mood I seem to be in on a particular evening determines the type of book I read. That reading goes on until I begin to get drowsy. Then the lights go off and I end the day with my own personal prayer. It has some of the elements of the morning prayer—intercession for family and friends, and thanks for the day. But it also has a bit of reflection on the events of the day and an acknowledgment that there were errors and missed opportunities for ministry. So the final part of my evening prayer is one of confession and seeking forgiveness.

Judy has her own pattern of following a lectionary for her evening Bible reading and then her own prayers. We are very private about our prayers and seldom discuss with each other the content of them.

I have gone to this length in sharing my own style of meditation, not to try to convince anyone that this is the "right" way of approaching meditation, but simply to illustrate in some detail how one person goes about it. And I certainly do not want to imply that I have achieved the peak of devotional life. To the contrary, I know that I am just a babe in the woods when it comes to meditation.

For one who is seeking to deepen one's prayer life and develop a pattern of meditation, the religious bookstores are well stocked with all manner of advice. A discussion of the subject among a group of the faithful is another source of help as people share the experiences of their own lives.

However, with prayer being such an important part of the lives of God's faithful people, I find it very strange that our churches have done so little to encourage and equip members in developing a more mature personal prayer life. Ask yourself: What has your pastor or congregational worship committee done in the past year to assist in your growth in daily personal prayer? When was the last time a course on prayer or the devotional life was offered in your adult education program at your church? How often does your congregation offer an adult retreat for the sole purpose of meditation and prayer?

In the narthex of our church there is always a stack of those little quarterly devotional booklets and occasionally an announcement is made encouraging people to use them. And once each year members of the congregation are asked to write a meditation which will become part of a Lenten devotional booklet that families are encouraged to use at dinnertime. We treasure this homemade devotional booklet much more than the professional one because it contains the thoughts and prayers of brothers and sisters in our congregation. But I have found that our congregation is more the exception than the rule in designing such a devotional aid. Most of the people I interviewed reported that their church has done nothing to encourage the personal prayer life of its members. For all practical purposes, the church institution has dismissed personal prayer and meditation as being not important in the lives of God's faithful people. Why?

We are back to dualism again. Our religious leaders have come to see the church as the center of the universe. It is only natural that they should feel thus. Their theological training was in a church-owned institution. Their professional careers usually begin in a church congregation. Some later move on to staff jobs in regional or national church offices, where some of them design worship and educational materials for use by laypersons. All of us speak and function out of our own experiences. And if our religious leaders' life experiences have been almost totally within the church, what would lead them to be concerned about how corporate prayer relates to a plant closing or how a corporate executive, faced with a plant closing, might find support for making a decision through personal prayer and private meditation? As a result, members of our congregations have tended to see prayer as more of a "churchy" activity than a worldly activity.

In his book *God's Lively People*, Mark Gibbs says, "Prayer is a stranger in the realm of work. It is not that men are unaware of the questions their work raises. They are probably worried about them more acutely than the clergy often think. But it never occurs to them that these questions have anything to do with prayer."[11] Gibbs's assertion is borne out by the fact, as stated earlier in this book, that none of the current "success" or "excellence" books, written by or about business persons, makes mention of the word "prayer." Not one.

But our survey of business executives does offer an important clue as to why the prayer life of most business persons does not relate to their work. When a person can honestly say that they feel called by God in their job, their prayer life is markedly different from the majority of persons who sense no such call. The problem is, so few business people sense a calling.

It is clear that prayer and meditation, both corporate and personal, are attributes of faithful Christians. But it is also clear that the church, by perpetuating dualism, does more harm than good in helping the faithful with their prayer lives.

SEVEN

LIFE IN COMMUNITY

It is 6:55 A.M. Outside it is still dark, but inside the diner the waitress is setting up a long table with sixteen places. A car pulls into the parking lot and the driver quickly makes his way through the light snow to the warmth of the dining room. Soon other cars appear and before long there are about fifteen people gathered around the long table, chatting and having their first cup of hot coffee. At a few minutes past seven, the group becomes silent as Will Boyer opens their meeting with a word of prayer. The waitress quickly takes each individual's order and disappears into the kitchen.

Dave, the leader for that day, passes out a sheet of paper on which he has presented a real-life case study of a problem he is facing in his work. The problem has to do with a deaf-mute he hired some years ago. Her job was to do the typesetting for his small advertising agency. Dave had a commitment to hire handicapped persons whenever he could and the typesetting job could be performed readily by a deaf-mute, thanks to computer technology. It was Sue's first job since she finished school. She was a bit slow at first, but because other members of the office staff could communicate with her through the computer network, she was able to do the work satisfactorily. Before long she was earning enough money to become independent of her family. She rented her own apartment and later bought her first car. Her sudden new independence was too much to handle, however. She began running around with a crowd that was into drugs and before long her work began to suffer. Dave tried to work with her and offered to pay for professional counseling. Sue refused. After having made several serious mistakes in her work, Sue managed to mess up one assignment so badly that Dave lost one of his major clients. He realized that he could do nothing more for Sue and so he let her go.

A few years passed and one day Dave got a call from Sue's mother. She told Dave how Sue had gone from one job to another and finally had to move back home. The mother assured Dave that Sue had learned a lesson and would he please give her a job again. It so happened at the time that Dave had an opening for a typesetter.

Dave's question at the bottom of his case study was: "As a Christian, what should I do?"

As the group read the case study, the waitress arrived with the food. People kept on reading as they ate their breakfasts. Finally, when it appeared that everyone had read the paper and had given some thought to Dave's situation, the discussion began. A number of questions were asked for further information. Did Dave have any assurance that Sue would be any better? How serious was the loss of the account? What specific things had Dave done to try to help Sue before he fired her? People were probing for possible strategies.

Then Dave pointed out, "You know, yesterday in church we had Holy Communion." He paused, "And in that sacrament I was totally forgiven by God for my failures." Looking down at his coffee cup and slowly shaking his head, he half whispered, "Am I not obligated to forgive the failures of others? Am I not obligated to hire Sue?"

Some agreed; others did not. People were obviously troubled with the way Dave put the final question. Is a Christian "obligated" to forgive other human beings, at the risk of being hurt by them again, simply because God freely forgives us? The pastor had several thoughts on the meaning of forgiveness. Various persons around the table suggested some possible actions Dave could take. No one pretended to have the definite solution, however. It was for Dave himself to decide.

By 8:00 A.M. the table was empty and the·fifteen persons were on their way to their various jobs as salespersons, managers, repairers, teachers, and government officials. The monthly meeting of The Monday Connection had adjourned. The Monday Connection is a group of people from the same congregation which meets the first Monday of each month to discuss the implications of being a Christian in their daily lives. I have been a part of the group for the past two years and have seen how God's presence has been experienced in the lives of people as they share their faith experiences with each other. Faithful people live in community with each other. That is clear.

In the previous chapter, we discussed the importance of listening for God as we engage in personal meditation and prayer. God can and does speak to us in these times of devotion. But God also speaks to us through our community of faith. As Dave listened to the questions and comments of his fellow church members that morning, he was hearing words from God. People were sharing with him their own experiences in the faith and their own perceptions of God's will. This is not to say that every word and every thought uttered that morning was a direct message from God, but it is to say that within that coming together of believers in the name of Jesus Christ was help for Dave in his search for direction. Jesus promised that "Where two or three are gathered in my name, there am I in the midst of them" (Matt. 18:20). We believe that.

Furthermore, if we believe in Jesus we believe in the incarnational principle. That is, we believe that the revelation of God comes to us through people. Not only have we received the revelation of God through Moses, the prophets, Jesus, Paul, and many other biblical greats, but we have continued to catch glimpses of our Creator through the ongoing train of Augustine, Saint Francis, Luther, Calvin, Bonhoeffer, King, and countless others. The incarnational principle suggests that revelations of God need not come exclusively from the great leaders of the Christian faith. The messages can come to us through any of God's faithful people. In fact, it is possible that God can speak to us through the words or actions of a nonbeliever. It would be a denial of the power of our Creator to claim that God can only be seen through the lives of those who qualify in some certain way.

But the incarnational principle does not work if we live in total isolation. We must be among people, we must be part of a community. The term "community" is generally meant to be a body of people having common interests or organization or living in the same place under the same laws.

Americans in the latter years of the twentieth century live in a variety of communities. First, there is the community of the family. But, where the family was once typically seen as a mother, father, and children living together for many years, the patterns have been changing. Today, more and more people choose not to marry and will describe their "family" in quite different terms. However defined, the family is one of the basic units of human community.

Beyond the family, we live in neighborhood communities and in political communities. We are members of a national community and of a global community. For many people the workplace represents another community. In fact, some persons are so wrapped up in their work that they are married to the company in a way that neglects all other community relationships. We may be members of any number of voluntary communities. I have watched with interest how our township volunteer fire department and paramedic unit has developed into a very tight community. Not only do they make serious commitments to the mission of the organization by being on call at all hours of the day, but they have broadened their task-oriented relationships into social relationships. They have their own clubhouse, dances, bazaars, meal service, and special events for members. On any night of the week, a member of the Cetronia Volunteer Fire Department can find warm friendship, acceptance, and a listening ear at the bar of the clubhouse attached to the fire station. Many of us also are members of communities of service clubs or political parties or special-interest groups. The list of opportunities for association with communities today is mind-boggling.

God's faithful people live in three types of communities at the same time: the universal community of faith, the congregation, and the relational or support community.

Starting some two thousand years ago, there has developed a worldwide community which claims to be the people of God and which confesses that it owes its existence to Jesus Christ. It spans both time and space. I am a member of the community of the early church at Philippi and Corinth and Rome. I am a member of the community of Saint Francis and Luther and Bonhoeffer. I am a member of the community of Christians in Japan and Germany, in Brazil and Ethiopia, in New York and Kansas City. One only has to travel to the local Christian communities in this country or abroad to appreciate the meaning of belonging to the universal community of faith.

Over the past fifteen years, I have done a good deal of traveling, mostly in this country but also in Europe, to help other Christians grasp the significance and potential of the ministry of the laity. I learned very early in these travels that while I could never be certain of the outcome of my efforts, I could be certain of one thing. I knew that when I walked in the door of that host community of faith, I would be totally accepted as one of them. There would be no need to prove my worthiness. I did not need to present credentials or letters of introduction. Simply because I was a member of the universal Christian community, I was welcomed by them and they were willing to listen to what I had to say. Yes, there were differences in religious practices, in theological interpretations, and in cultural patterns, but that was secondary to our relationship to each other as members of the universal community of Christians. The assurance of acceptance within the universal community is unlike anything else I have experienced as a member of a variety of other organizations.

Unfortunately, for many there is not the opportunity to experience this sense of a universal community of Christians. We may be aware of it and we may believe it exists, but, until we actually experience it, we cannot appreciate the exhilaration of membership in it.

For most Christians in the USA today the local congregation is the primary, and sometime only, expression of Christian community. From all the survey work I did and from all the interviews, it was clear that faithfulness involves an ongoing association with an organized community of Christians. Of the business persons surveyed for this book, 92.4% considered themselves to be active members of their congregations. Of those who feel a sense of calling and a sense of ministry in their lives, the response was virtually 100%.

While we commonly think of Jesus as traveling from town to town with a small band of disciples, it is interesting to note the frequency with which the Gospel writers report of his teaching in the synagogues or temple. Matthew records five such instances, Mark tells of six, Luke reports on twelve, and John cites six. In fact, Luke indicates that it was a common practice of Jesus to teach "in their synagogues" (4:15), and to go into the synagogue on the Sabbath day, "as his custom was" (4:16). While Jesus was at times very sharp in his criticism of the religious leaders of his day, he did recognize and associate with local communities of faith.

The local congregation has played a crucial role in my own pilgrimage of faith. My mother and father were married in St. Michael's Lutheran Church. I was baptized in Christ Lutheran Church and learned about the Bible and the life of Jesus in its Sunday school. I was taught Lutheran doctrine as a catechumen by a professional who had been educated in a Lutheran seminary and who had been officially called and ordained by the Lutheran church to do such teaching, among other things. I received the sacrament of Holy Communion for the first time in that church. And I participated regularly in a worship service that was designed with a specific order and flow by ones who also had received specialized training in the colleges and seminaries of the church. Yes, there were some negatives, but these positive contributions to my development as a Christian were absolutely essential and would not have happened, at least not for me, had there been no local congregation.

Very frankly, I did not experience a sense of Christian community as a young person, nor did I respond to my faith through Christian action in my life. For a period of about five years, as a teenager, I completely divorced myself from the church. Yet, its imprint on my life had been made.

It was not until years later, in a different congregation in Detroit, that I first began to experience the kind of love and caring which can exist within the local congregation. I still recall the time when Judy hovered near death in Henry Ford Hospital. There I was with three small children, six hundred miles away from any family members. Judy's sister, Sally, rushed from the East to be with us, but it was the countless meals which came to our front door and the assurances of prayer from members of our congregation that gave me my first real taste of life in Christian community. It was our sponsorship of refugees from East Germany that gave me my first taste of Christian action within a local community of faith. And it was the "couples' club" that gave me my first taste of a small Christian support group.

By not dwelling more on the importance of active involvement of Christians in their local congregation, I do not want to diminish its importance. Rather, I would like to assume that there is consensus that, of course, faithfulness involves active membership in a local, organized community of faith. There is no evidence to the contrary. That is the good news.

The bad news, however, is that for most Christians the local congregation is their *only* experience of Christian community. It is bad news for several reasons. First, many Christian congregations in this country are essentially dead.

Paul is the president and chief executive officer of a major corporation. Like me, he was brought up by a Christian family and was educated in a Lutheran congregation. His children were raised within the life of that congregation and he passionately wants his grandchildren to be members of some local congregation. "But, Bill," he says to me with a sigh of despair, "my church life is dead. Stale. I absolutely get nothing out of a worship service anymore. I don't understand it. I believe in the church, yet nothing is happening when I sit there on a Sunday morning."

I know what Paul means. As I visit in other congregations, as a guest speaker or conference leader, it is very depressing to observe the drabness and lack of enthusiasm within so many worship services. "Why do these people keep coming back here?" I find myself asking. In some instances, the answer is that they do not come back, as evidenced by so many empty seats in these huge church buildings.

Frequently, I have been on the receiving end of lectures about people who claim they "don't get anything out of church anymore." The chastisement is based on the premise that people should be coming to church to give rather than to receive. They should be coming, so the argument goes, to give thanks, to make confession, to give praise to God. If we give something in our worship services, we will begin to get something out of them, says the lecturer. Perhaps, but does that not fly in the face of a theology that says it is God who is the initiator of our relationship with God and we act in response to God's gift of grace? Can our right practices in a church service merit a meaningful worship experience any more than our right deeds in life merit eternal salvation? I do not think the argument is theologically defensible. Of course we give in our worship services but there has to be the sense of God's action within that experience also.

In his essay on "Conversion Within the Church," Elton Trueblood focuses on the large number of nominal church members who have never really been brought into a committed relationship with Christ. He argues that the greatest field for Christian evangelism today is *in* the church. He writes, "The task before us is clear. The task is to try to reach the present membership of churches with a message of such vitality that they experience a conversion within the church, rather than a conversion to the church."[1]

There can be a variety of reasons why the message of vitality is not getting through in many congregations. It is not true that the fault always lies with the pastor. I know of many cases where a vibrant, dedicated, and skilled pastor is being ground down by a congregation that has grown to like being dead. At the same time, I know many cases where the pastor *is* the problem. The point here is not to examine why some congregations are alive and some are dead. The point simply is to state that if one's only experience in Christian community is one's local congregation and it happens to be a dead one, the only remaining option is to seek out a lively congregation. And, since most people in such a circumstance do not know what they are missing, there is no reason to look elsewhere.

A second reason why it is not desirable to have the local congregation as one's only point of Christian community has to do with size. Most congregations need to have several hundred members in order to be viable. How does one relate in an experiential way to a hundred other persons? The brief encounters we have with others as we come and go from Sunday worship services hardly lend themselves to sharing one's faith experiences. And when the congregation does break the larger group into smaller units it is usually for a specific task. The church council meets not in order to support the faith of each other, but to do the work of running the organization. Same with all the committees of the congregation. They meet to do their assigned tasks, not to be a place where people share questions about how one relates faith to daily life. Sometimes the choir can become a small Christian community, but usually it is by accident rather than by intent.

Adult study groups have the potential for becoming support groups, but too often the leader is more intent upon covering a predetermined amount of material than upon allowing people to engage in conversation which may spring out of one individual's need or concern. Unless a congregation intentionally provides for small Christian support groups, it is more than likely that most of its members will never experience a kind of Christian community that was typical of the early church. There simply is no chance to interact with other Christians on a very personal level.

A third reason why the local congregation should not be one's only point of Christian community is the problem of dualism mentioned earlier. All organizations, including the local congregation, depend on the support of members for survival. By "involving" as many members of the congregation as possible in the work of the congregation, the organization assures its own survival. The focus for Christian service then becomes service to the congregation instead of service to the world. There seems to be an assumption that if everybody is very active in congregational life, if the choir sings well, if the church-school teachers are fully recruited, if all the committees are well staffed with volunteers, then the people of God in that congregation will move from Sunday worship into weekday ministry. Except, it does not happen because the focus is in the wrong direction.

Take Sunday, for instance. Despite the fact that our calendars show Sunday as the first day of the week, our church activities point to Sunday as the culmination of the week. Sermons are prepared for the Sunday worship service. Choirs rehearse for Sunday. Church-school teachers ready their lessons for Sunday. The sexton is especially busy, cleaning in preparation for Sunday. And when noon comes on Sunday and the last "Amen" is sounded, everyone breathes a sigh of relief. Now they can have a few days of relaxation before getting ready for the next Sunday.

How often is the question asked, "What is happening in the lives of our people on Monday as a result of what we did on Sunday?" Hardly ever. Why? Because we have come to see the Sunday worship experience as an end in itself, rather than a means to an end. In theory, the people of God "congregate" on a Sunday morning for worship, study, the sacraments, prayer, and inspiration *so that* they can go into the world on Monday as ministers of Jesus Christ. Yet, as someone has pointed out, the army of Christ is constantly being encouraged to stay in the barracks for more training.

When my book *Thank God, It's Monday!*[2] first came out, it was assumed that it was a book for pastors. After all, who else would be thankful it is Monday? Even today, when I talk to people about the need for Christians to see that the Monday world is their arena for mission and ministry, many people respond, "That's an interesting thought!"

The Monday Connection breakfast, referred to at the start of this chapter, was so titled simply because we wanted to see what connection there was between the Sunday worship service we had the day before and the weekday problem being brought to us by one of our members. The fact that there were so many times when the presenter of the case study could make *no* connection with the Sunday worship service has caused our pastor to experiment with new forms and styles of Sunday worship.

The reason Paul, the president of a major company, found church to be "dead" was because it was not relating in any way to the experiences of his life. In a sense, he found himself in two worlds which did not connect. The world of his company, fighting for its survival, was alive and dynamic. The world of church, with no apparent connection to his weekday world, was irrelevant.

For all these reasons, it is necessary, I am convinced, for God's faithful people also to be a part of a smaller community of Christians which can add a different dimension to their faith lives. The small Christian support group can supply that which the larger congregation cannot.

We need to remind ourselves that Jesus was very intentional about the support group of twelve which were a part of his ministry. He selected twelve very ordinary men to follow him. They became the core group for his mission. He taught them, empowered them, and sent them on missions. At times, he asked them for feedback. ("Who do people say that the son of man is?" Matt. 16:13.) He asked for presence and support in the garden of Gethsemane while he prayed over his forthcoming death. The Gospel writers tell us of many occasions when the crowds pressed in and followed him. Yet, he maintained the core group of twelve. While there were many who knew Jesus personally, it was the group of twelve that came to know him best of all.

During the interviews, it became apparent that while only a small number of the people I talked to were members of small Christian support groups, everyone who was claimed that it was an absolutely essential part of their lives. Some said that they actually had a conversion experience as a result of their small group community.

In the introduction to the book *Growth Through Groups,* Findley B. Edge says this about his own experiences in his first small group:

> I came to be aware in a deeper way than I had ever known before of God's love for me and his acceptance of me as I was (though always desiring better things for me). The people in that small group knew

me as I was with my failures, my weaknesses, my struggles, and yet they loved me. This was a rather overwhelming experience for me because I had always lived my life (as evidently many people do) with the feeling that if people knew me as I really was they would not like me. . . . But these people knew me as I was (or at least a lot better than anyone had ever known me before) and yet they still loved me. It was through this type of relationship that I became more deeply aware that God, who knew me as I was, could also love me. . . . Not only did I come to know at a deeper level what it meant to be loved, I also came to know, through "incarnation," what it meant to love others. Because of the searching, sharing, praying we did together, because of the relationships we experienced together, I came to love the members of this group in a way that I have never loved people before, outside of my immediate family. I really came to know these people. I knew where they ached. I knew where they struggled. I knew their deep yearnings. I knew the particular points where they were striving to change and to grow. I prayed daily for each one of them by name.[3]

Dr. Edge pointed out that he learned about the *concept* of koinonia, or Christian community, in the seminary. It was in his head. "But it was with this group," he adds, "in relationship that I came closer to experiencing what I think New Testament koinonia is like than ever before in my life."[4]

To Findley's words I can only say, "Ditto and Amen!" Those are my exact sentiments. I doubt very much that I would still be a church member today if it had not been for the experiences that have enriched my own life through the many small groups we were in over the past thirty years.

The words "relationships" and "experiences" keep popping up when one talks about the small-group movement. It is in the small group where we can relate to people at a far deeper level than we can with a much larger body of Christians. And it is in the small group that we are able to share our life's experiences and to support each other in new and troublesome ventures in a way which would be impossible with a very large group.

THE SMALL-GROUP EXPERIENCE

It is not the purpose of this chapter to go into lengthy explanations of what small groups are like and how to form them. There are already many good resources available for that. Let me briefly describe the typical small group to which our family related over the past thirty years. It is a composite picture of six different support groups.

The group consisted of between twelve and twenty adults. Most were married couples, but singles were also represented. Most often, but not always, we were from the same congregation. We met every other Friday evening in our homes, taking turns at being the host. For those members who did not have a space at home that would accommodate as many as eighteen to twenty people, there was an understanding that they were not expected to be hosts. We gathered promptly at 8:00 P.M. and we always adjourned promptly at 10:00 P.M. The host usually had coffee and perhaps a piece of pie as we settled in. By about 8:15 or so, the host would lead the group in a brief period of meditation. Sometimes it was a scripture reading. Sometimes it was a reading from a devotional booklet. Sometimes we listened to music. The host then led us in prayer. For each evening there had been a topic assigned. It may have been a chapter from a book the group had been studying. It may have been an issue of current social concern. But before we got into the study portion of the evening, the host always provided an opportunity for sharing. If someone had a special piece of good news or a special item of concern, the group was told about it. If a member had a problem they wanted to share with the others, the topic for the evening was put aside and we dealt with that person's immediate need. Otherwise, we began the study period.

The study topic always related in some way to contemporary Christian living. It might have been on a current issue of the times or it might have been a book of theology. But it always related faith to life. While there frequently were intellectual discussions, we tried very hard to bring our personal feelings and experiences into the discussions. Of course, after you have been with a small group twice a month for over five years, you get to know what each individual's reactions to a particular issue will be. But we have learned that through the sharing of our own personal perspectives, we do gain new insights that bring about change in our own opinions. While there was the freedom to argue with each other, we were sensitive to the feelings of others and seldom indulged in "letting it all hang out," as the transactional groups encouraged during the 1960s.

About once a month, we had a family dinner together to which all our children were invited. There were also Christmas parties, ice skating events, bowling, picnics, and other social events in which we participated as total families. Once a year, we all went on a weekend retreat, as total families. The program was usually designed by a committee of members. It was these many family events that brought our children into the community life. And over a period of time, we discovered that certain children were developing strong affinities to other adults in the group. That suited us fine.

We supported each other in illnesses, divorces, problems with children, deaths of parents, and losses of jobs. When a family had a new baby baptized, we all sat together in the church service as the baby's extended family. When the first child in the group was married, we were all there in the family section.

One of our groups started a fair-housing committee in a time and place when such activities were frowned upon. In fact, it came about because our church council refused to have our congregation associated with fair housing and one member suggested I resign if I continued with my work. Our small group provided the means for an ecumenical fair-housing committee to become established.

Another of our small groups sponsored a family of eighteen Ugandan refugees. We did it because local congregations were afraid to take the risk.

Without any doubt, the experiences we have shared with other Christians in our support groups as we moved around the country blossomed into the richest Christian relationships we have known. We still keep in contact with two of the families from Detroit in the 1950s. At least twice a year, we get together with three of the families from our 1960s stay in Devon, Pennsylvania. One of those annual events is regularly an overnight visit at our summer home in the Poconos.

Although our patterns have changed, we still participate with a support group we started in Allentown fourteen years ago. At the same time, we have been a part of newer ones which have started in our present congregation.

The major criticism of small support groups comes from pastors and those who see no need for them. Since the pastor in most congregations is held accountable for everything that happens there, it is difficult for some clergy to permit a group to exist which he or she cannot control. The argument is that it is divisive (one theologian said it was "heresy") to have a "church within a church," as it is described. Yet my experience has been that our small groups are not in competition with the larger congregation, nor do they represent a splinter group. To the contrary, in most cases the members of our small groups have been active leaders in the congregation.

Some people criticize the small groups for being cliques. In every group I have been in we were careful to make known that anyone who was interested was invited to join. In thirty years there was only one instance in which a person joined who was so disruptive that we had to ask him to leave. And, in response to the charges of cliques, I resonate with Findley Edge who writes, "I had rather have some cliques in my church where the participants really love each other, than to have the usual kind of church fellowship where we slap each other on the back, drink punch together, carry on casual conversation, but do not care for one another on any depth level."[5] To which I must add that it has been through the experience of love and acceptance that I have come to know in a small group that I have been able to risk being more loving and accepting of others outside the group.

It is interesting to note that Jesus, who was very intentional about selecting a small group of twelve, is never accused of starting a clique. In fact, he had a core within the core. On a number of occasions he took Peter, James, and John with him and left the other nine behind. Was he being "cliquish"?

While small support communities have been so powerful in the lives of those who have experienced them, the sad truth is that most Christians have had no such relationships with others. In the survey I conducted among business leaders, "participating in a religiously oriented support group" came in dead last in percentage of activities that the respondents regularly do. Active church membership got a 92.4% yes vote, but support groups got only 16.7% who claim regular participation. Even among those who claimed a sense of calling in their jobs, only 24% regularly participated in religiously oriented support groups. Why are so few business persons in support groups?

One must keep in mind the environment that exists within the business community. A few years ago, Michael Maccoby, in his book

The Gamesman,[6] pointed out that the nature of corporate management today is such that one is rewarded for qualities of the head (careerism, initiative, coolness under stress, creativity, etc.) but not qualities of the heart (compassion, generosity, friendliness, idealism, etc.). I think that situation still prevails today, perhaps more so than in 1976. Accordingly, business leaders are conditioned to be very wary of getting into situations where they may be asked to share their feelings with others or to relate to others at a deep level. So, both the sacred and the secular world of the business person are at work to keep him or her away from one of the most enriching experiences a Christian can have—to be a member of a small intimate community of faith.

There is a sad PS to all this for the business person. One part of the survey asked, "When faced with a troubling problem in your occupation, to what extent do you turn to the following for help in discussing it?" "The family" was the most frequently cited source of support, but only 39.2% of the respondents always turned to their family. In second place were "colleagues at work," but only 27.5% of the business people always turned to them. In third place was the category "friends away from work," with only 6.5% always consulting them. In fourth place came the respondent's pastor, with only 4.7% always seeking this support. In dead last was the professional counselor at 0%!

I firmly believe that if business people can be brought into Christian support groups much will happen in their faith lives. The small group will be their linkage between Sunday faith and weekday life. I know from experience that it is true.

Being in Christian community is one of the marks of faithfulness. Christian community takes three expressions: the universal community, the local congregation, and the koinonia or small Christian support group. If one does not have a sense of affiliation with all three, one is missing something important in this pilgrimage of faith.

EIGHT

THE GIVERS

Some time ago I heard a pastor talk about "giving" using an analogy based on the two seas in Israel. It went something like this:

> There are two seas in the Holy Land. The one is called the Sea of Galilee. It is a sea of sparkling blue waters. Its banks are lined with trees. Birds can be heard singing. Children play in its waters and fish abound. It provides irrigation for rich farmland for miles around and drinking water for many towns. The Sea of Galilee receives its waters from the River Jordan in the north, and discharges water into the River Jordan in the south.
>
> The other sea is dark and murky. No trees or birds can be found along its banks. Its oily saltwater is unfit to drink. No farms or towns can be found near its shores. It, too, receives water in the north from the River Jordan. But it does not discharge any water it receives. All is lost through evaporation and so it has collected heavy deposits of salts and minerals over the centuries. It is called the Dead Sea.
>
> The difference between the two seas is this: The Sea of Galilee receives and gives its water. The Dead Sea receives and keeps its water. The Sea of Galilee is alive; the other sea is dead.
>
> There are two kinds of people in the world: those who receive and give and those who receive and keep. The one kind are alive; the others are dead.

As I conducted interviews in our search for faithfulness, it was in the area of giving that most people felt it was easiest to perceive God's faithful people. "Just because someone goes to church you can't assume they are among God's faithful," said Paul, "but if they are giving people you can be sure they have been touched by God." I pressed him further on this by asking if he felt the same about non-Christians who give to others. He replied, "I don't care if they are Christians or Jews or Moslems or what. A person who gives to others is a person touched by God." Most others seemed to agree. Faithful people are marked by their willingness to give to others, be it their time, their abilities, or their money.

Much has been said and written in recent years about the way American society has drifted into a style of individualism in which the attitude is "what's in it for me?" Many sociologists proclaim that we are increasingly a nation of self-centered people. They point out that marriage, which involves a commitment to another person, is less stable than it was fifty years ago. Young people are delaying marriage more frequently in order to acquire more material security or attain certain career goals. Linda, a professional family counselor, tells me that many young couples are very frank in their reasons for not wanting to have children: "Children cost too much," they say. Fewer marriages are surviving because one or both partners did not get out of the relationship what they had anticipated.

For a number of years the Yankelovich, Skelly and White organization has been doing public-opinion research which is used by sponsoring companies to guide them in consumer trends. Over the years, the trend has been more and more toward the purchase of "me" items, such as clothing, perfume, jewelry, and the like, and less on "we" items such as family-room furniture and family games.

During the 1960s, I was frequently invited, as a representative of corporate management, to meet with college students in seminars on business. I was always on the defensive as the students expressed criticism of the greed and materialism they perceived in business. They scoffed at the living style of corporate America and demanded that we be more concerned about societal and environmental issues.

Today I teach business ethics at a local college and am constantly astonished by how determined so many of our young people are to make it "big" in their careers. They have abiding faith in the self-correcting nature of the free-enterprise system and are willing to give corporate America the benefit of the doubt whenever some wrong-doing is uncovered. They do not wish to rock the boat.

Now, in fairness to our young people, it must be remembered that the 1960s were boom years when jobs were awaiting all college graduates. It was easy to be critical of corporate America if one was certain to find employment in another field. Today's college students do not have as certain a promise as they follow behind the huge "baby boom" which has largely met the needs of the job market.

Nevertheless, even if one takes into consideration that job prospects have changed, there is still an undeniable difference between the youth of the sixties and those of the eighties. The focus is more on what I can get than on what I can give.

Business ethicists today are debating whether there is more unethical conduct in business and industry today or whether we are simply more aware of it. Writing in a recent issue of *New York* magazine, Bernice Kanner describes "today's go-go ethics" as an obsession with riches which is unparalleled in our history. Citing case after case of wrongdoing in business, government, and society in general, she claims that the overall mood among ethics professionals is gloomy. She quotes sociology professor Joseph Bensman, of the City University of New York, as predicting that it may take "a depression or something that produces a general epic of service before things get better."[1]

Writing about the flood of scandals in the investment industry, Myron Magnet, a staff writer for *Fortune* magazine, puts it this way:

> They have their own ethic, and it centers on money, as is increasingly true for the ethic of the culture at large. "Where we saw in the Sixties the nation of public service, in the Eighties money is the thing," says Harvard's Samuel Hayes. For the get-rich-quick mergers and acquisition generation, it sometimes seems that money is the only value. "The people with the most money are admired regardless of how they achieved it," says James Schreiber, a New York lawyer who specializes in cases involving securities fraud. The investment banking boom gives these people their chance to be rich and they are taking it.[2]

The issue of individualism and commitment in American life is the focus of a recent best-selling book, *Habits of the Heart* by Robert N. Bellah. Reminding us that as early as the 1830s, Tocqueville observed that democracy itself fosters an individualism which undermines commitments to others, the authors present an interesting history of the American struggle to find a middle ground between self and community. In their concluding chapter the authors state, "The litmus test that both the biblical and republican traditions give us for assaying the health of a society is how it deals with the problem of wealth and poverty."[3]

How we deal with wealth and poverty are certainly within the tradition of our Bible and our republican form of government. The United States has had a remarkable history of its people volunteering time and money to serve the needs of its less fortunate citizens. No other nation in the world has had as many volunteer agencies in which people personally give of themselves for the benefit of others.

In 1985, according to Independent Sector, 89 million Americans 14 years of age or older (48 percent of this population) reported volunteering an average of 3.5 hours per week, totaling 16.1 billion hours for the year.[4] Volunteering for religious organizations accounts for 19% of this time, while the fields of health and education are tied for second place with 12% each of all time contributed by volunteers. Recreation accounted for 7%, while community action, citizenship, and general fund-raising each represented 6%.

The same Independent Sector report indicated that, in 1984, 89% of all Americans gave to charity. Their giving level averaged out at $650 per reporting household, which represents 2.4% of total household incomes. Another study done by Independent Sector in 1984 revealed a surprising pattern of giving. People with incomes below $10,000 in 1981 contributed 3.85% of their money to charity, while those in the $50,000 to $100,000 range contributed only 1.35%. More astonishing was the revelation that families with incomes of $5,000 or less contributed about 5% of their annual income.[5]

As in the case of donation of time, religious organizations were the primary beneficiaries of financial gifts, with 46.5% of the total going to them. Educational institutions received 14.5%, health and hospitals accounted for 13.9%, social welfare received 10.5%, and the arts and humanities got 8.2%.[6]

It is true that volunteering exists in other countries of the world, but nowhere else have the numbers, proportions, and impact been so great.

But there are ominous signs on the horizon. Younger people are not volunteering their time or their money to the degree that they did a decade ago. Brian O'Connell, president of Independent Sector, writes, "There are clear signs that citizenship participation and community service may not be as vital a part of our society for the younger generation and those who come after them."[7]

The 1980s witnessed many attacks upon government-financed programs for the poor, the elderly, and children. While there is little question that some of the programs had been abused and were ineffective, it became popular to scoff at almost all government programs except the military. Writing in the July 20, 1986, issue of the *Washington Post*, John Hess comments on the way many younger people are turning against social security: "In 1936 we willingly began to tax our mostly wretched wages to guarantee the elderly a dignified retirement with the explicit assurance that if the payroll tax yield was not enough, the general revenues would be tapped for the difference." He adds, "I was a youth when Social Security was enacted in 1935 and I am shocked by the change in climate. The country was desperately poor then, yet we adopted a feast of generous legislation. Now the country is rich, and mean."[8]

Yet, in the face of all these trends toward increased individualism, increased materialism, and decreased concern for others, the people I interviewed for this book maintain that faithful people are different. They say that God's faithful people continue to give of their time, their skills, and their money for the sake of those who have needs. Dorothy put it this way: "It's impossible to be a follower of Jesus and not to be a giving person. He gave of himself, even to the point of giving his life. If you are truly his follower, you must be a giving person also."

The Gospel accounts of Jesus' ministry do indeed record a steady stream of accounts of Jesus giving to those in need. His power to heal physical disabilities and to restore life brought throngs of needy persons into his presence. Matthew tells us of twenty-one different occasions when he healed someone. Mark tells of seventeen occasions, Luke cites twenty-one, and John mentions five. Jesus gave the multitudes food and, within the power granted to him by God, he gave many forgiveness. His teachings were rich with admonitions to his followers to give. "Freely you have received, freely give," he told his disciples as he sent them out (Matt. 10:8 NIV). In the Sermon on the Mount, he tells the crowd, "Give to the one who asks you, and do not turn away from the one who wants to borrow from you" (Matt. 5:42 NIV).

Jesus saw the love of money as a stumbling block for those who would seek to follow him. The encounter with the rich ruler is the best example. In response to the ruler's question of what he had to do to inherit eternal life, Jesus reminded him of the Commandments. The ruler responded that he had obeyed them all since he was a boy. When Jesus heard this, he said to him, "One thing you still lack. Sell all that you have and distribute to the poor, and you will have treasure in heaven; and come, follow me" (Luke 18:22). The ruler went away sad because the order to give away everything and to follow Jesus was more than he could accept.

A short time later, Luke tells us of the reverse side of the failure of the ruler to give his all when he praises the poor widow who put two very small copper coins in the temple treasury while the rich were putting in considerably more. Jesus says, "This poor widow has put in more than all of them; for they all contributed out of their abundance, but she out of her poverty put in all the living that she had" (Luke 21:3–4). In the parable of the Rich Man and Lazarus (Luke 16:19), Jesus tells the story of a rich man condemned to hell because he ignored the beggar, Lazarus, who lay at his gate.

Note that Jesus' concern for giving is not only focused on the needs of the poor, but also on the need of the giver to give. He did not appeal to the rich ruler to give for the benefit of the poor, but rather to give for his own benefit.

Furthermore, both the Old and the New Testaments speak of a discipline of giving which involves first-fruits giving and proportionate giving. Exodus 22 and 23 indicate that it is the firstborn of the cattle and sheep and the crops which are to be offered to God. Moreover, giving was to be one-tenth of one's gain. "All the tithe of the land, whether of the seed of the land or of the fruit of the trees, is the Lord's; it is holy to the Lord" (Lev. 27:30). The same principles of proportionate giving and first-fruits giving were part of the life of the early church. Paul writes to the church at Corinth, "On the first day of every week, each of you is to put something aside and store it up, as he may prosper, so that contributions need not be made when I come" (1 Cor. 16:2).

In the survey of Lutheran business executives, 82.7% claimed to be practicing proportionate giving and 31.5% indicated that they tithed. This response indicates a level of commitment to giving which is well above average among all Lutherans. Once again, however, when the responses of those who sense a call from God in their occupations are compared to the responses of those who do not, there is a significant difference. Among those who sense a call, 92.2% practice proportionate giving and 52% tithe. The acknowledgment of our faithful relationship with God continues to produce more positive responses to the various marks of faithfulness.

Because the religious institutions of America are totally dependent upon the voluntary contributions of their members, they have worked hard at encouraging people to give. That they have succeeded to a remarkable degree is borne out by the statistics of the Independent Sector reports cited earlier in the chapter. Religious organizations get the largest single share of volunteer time and, by far, the largest share of money donated by the American public.

This need to raise money to support the churches of our land has a reverse side to it, however. It reinforces the dualistic nature of religion in America. In the fall of every year, no matter where we were living, we received materials from our congregation calling upon us to consider our financial commitment to the work of the church. October or November is "Stewardship Month." There are letters written, sermons preached, people visited, speeches made, all on behalf of Christian giving. We are reminded of the many biblical admonitions to give and to give cheerfully. We are reminded of the biblical concept of stewardship. We are stewards of what God has given us and we ought to exercise that stewardship by contributing liberally to our church. People are urged to practice proportionate giving and to make the tithe a minimum goal. The message has come through so often and so strong that if you ask people what is meant by the term "Christian giving" they will immediately say that it refers to giving to your church. And that is where the dualism comes in.

The Bible talks about giving to the poor, the widow, the orphan, as well as giving to the religious organization. Nowhere is the message of giving more clearly articulated than in John 3:16: "For God so loved the world that he gave his only Son . . . " It *does not read*, "For God so loved the *church* . . ." Yet, year after year, we reinforce the principle that good stewardship of our finances means giving money to the church. While this is true, not a word is said about giving to the world.

I am forever grateful to Walter Fisher and Russ Jensen who came to our home in Detroit in 1951 after we joined a Lutheran church there. They were from a stewardship committee and wanted to talk to Judy and me about proportionate giving. They brought with them a little plastic box on which was inscribed the words "Lord's

Treasury." They spoke of the need of Christians to give because of the manner in which God constantly gives to us. They said that they had been using the Lord's Treasury for a number of years and that it was a wonderful experience for them.

The plan was simple: We would commit to putting a fixed percent of our income into the box on every payday. That money was to be considered belonging to God and was to be used in whatever manner we felt Christ would want us to apply it. If we felt that God would want it all to go to the church to which we belonged, fine. But if we saw someone in need or knew of a worthy cause that needed money, the Lord's Treasury money could be used there also. Whatever direction that money went was to be an expression of how we best saw God's will being done.

They suggested that we start at whatever giving level we had at that time and by some plan that we would be comfortable with increase our percent giving level regularly until we reached a minimum of 10 percent of gross income. I liked the part of deciding how the money could best be used, but I sure gulped at the figure of 10 percent. Some quick calculations showed me that we were only at about a 1.5 percent level at the time.

Walter Fisher and Russ Jensen were not a couple of slick, fast-talking salesmen. They merely shared with Judy and me their very deep conviction that the Lord's Treasury was a very important part of their lives. Their sincerity was captivating. So we said we would do it. We decided to go to a 2.5 percent level of giving immediately, and we agreed to ourselves that every time I got a raise from that day on we would increase our giving level 1 percent until we reached the tithe. At the time it truly seemed like a scary thing to do. As a young family just getting started in a new job in a strange city and with a very tight budget, it seemed to be a daring thing that we were about to do. As it turned out, it was a cakewalk. Between cost-of-living increases and merit increases, I received two or three raises a year and within a few years we were at the 10-percent level. And there always was more than enough money for us to live on after we put aside the first 10 percent. But by far the most exciting part of the program was the disbursing of that money. First, we decided as a matter of principle that God probably would not want us to be giving more than half of our Lord's treasury to the local church. And because the world is the object of God's love, our use of that money should take into consideration the needs of all creation. And so, we carefully looked at all kinds of charitable appeals and were attentive to needs that surfaced within our community and nation.

It was a very liberating factor in our lives also. If the doorbell rang and there was someone there soliciting money for a particular charity or cause, our response was based on our judgment of the need. Since the money was already in our Lord's Treasury, awaiting our use of it, we never again felt guilty saying no to a cause for reason of feeling we needed to keep our money. Prior to this time, if I would refuse to give to a cause, I would feel guilty about my stinginess. With the Lord's Treasury the money was already there and I could freely say no, based on my judgment as to whether it was the best use of money we had put aside to give in the name of Jesus Christ.

As our children grew, we had many family meetings on how best to use the Lord's Treasury money. We would actually set the plastic box on our dining-room table and count the money that had accumulated there since last we talked about giving. And then we would decide where we felt Jesus would best want that money used. How much should go to the Christian Children's Fund for some orphan in Korea? How much for a hunger appeal? How about the United Negro College Fund? The United Way? Meals on Wheels? As a family we decided on the priorities.

All four of our children are now adults and they are all giving people. I am convinced that it was the way in which they saw us giving in proportion to our receiving that got them into the style of being giving people.

In later years, I have tried to encourage other congregations in which we have been members to undertake the Lord's Treasury program. None has done it and, frankly, the fear is that it will decrease the level of giving to the church if we encourage people to look at the wider range of Christian giving.

Franklin is the president of a small business in our town. He is an active churchgoing person. His business has prospered and Franklin is living a very comfortable life. He has been very generous in his giving to the church and its institutions. I know he is a large giver to our seminary, our church-related college, and several of our church-related social service agencies. I happened to get his card to call upon him for a corporate gift to the United Way. When I saw the low level of corporate gift he had been making to the United Way in past years, I was shocked. Not only was the gift a token one, but he did not even permit United Way volunteers to talk to his workers about their contributions to that cause. When I talked to him about the United Way, it became apparent that he had no complaints about the organization or what it did. He thought it was a fine organization. It was not a matter of being negative on the United Way. It was simply that he had been so conditioned to giving to the church *only* that he never considered that Christian giving might also include giving to nonchurch needs. He had been educated to believe that Christian giving meant giving to the church, period. Score another victory for dualism.

But there is another part of this stewardship business that the church ignores. With the concentration on encouraging its members to become tithers and give 10 percent of their income to the church, whatever is said about the other 90 percent? Does God only care about what I give to the church? Or does stewardship involve all of my possessions, all of my money? Is it O.K. to live extravagantly as long as I give 10 percent to the church? Is it agreeable to God that I indulge myself and my family with expensive creature comforts so long as I fork over a tithe to my church? Is that really Christian stewardship?

From time to time, I will hear a sermon in which the ethics of how money is made in America is discussed. What about the ethics of how I spend the money I earn? How many sermons do we hear about this?

We can be ashamed of the narrow, self-serving manner in which Christian giving and Christian stewardship are presented in our churches today. I am aware of the fear some may have that if they really talk about stewardship of life, people will be giving more elsewhere and less to their church. That belief is dead wrong! It is wrong because it is theologically indefensible and it is wrong because it does not play out that way in real life. Every faithful person I know who has come to see stewardship in its broadest, richest dimensions is a strong financial supporter of his or her congregation. I know of no exceptions.

The narrowness of thinking goes beyond the stewardship of money, unfortunately. A few years ago, I came across a little article titled "God's Time" in a denominational newspaper. The pastor who wrote it did an analysis of how we spend the hours of the week. Fifty-six hours went toward sleep, 50 toward work, 17 toward eating, and so on. At the bottom of his list of activities he had 2.5 hours devoted to God through Sunday worship and any daily prayers we may say. This amounted to about 1.5 percent of our time. He called it "God's Time." "Is this all we care about God?" he thundered. Laying a real guilt trip on all the readers, the pastor argued for greater involvement in weekday worship services and congregational activities. Once more the implication was plain: God cares only about the time we devote to activities in our church. None of the rest of our time is of concern to God. Not that volunteering at the hospital, not that literacy teaching, not that driving meals-on-wheels, not that community youth work. Only things done at church.

While the pastor's article is perhaps a worst-case example, it is nevertheless true that many church members feel guilty about saying no to some volunteer work in the congregation simply because they are too busy with volunteer work in the community. How often do our congregations recognize and celebrate all the hours of volunteer time given by its members in service to others in the community?

I recently received a letter from a pastor in which he described the makeup of his congregation. He wrote, "This is a very talented congregation. We have many outstanding people both in their churchmanship and in their work in the world." He closed the note to me with the words, "They are also, unfortunately, extremely busy people." I knew immediately that the "unfortunate" aspect of his parishioners' lives referred to their work in the world, not to their churchmanship. Never have I heard a pastor or lay congregational leader express regret that someone was too busy with their work in the church.

It is truly shameful that the Christian churches of today have been so narrow in their treatment of Christian giving and Christian service. If anything, they have obstructed Christian growth and development among the faithful. By reinforcing a concept that we live in two worlds, the church is thwarting the mission and ministry of God's people. How can the incarnational principle of God being active through God's people happen in this hungry world if the churches so distort the ministry of the laity? But, thanks to the Holy Spirit, there are people out there filled with the love of God, giving of their time, talents, and financial resources, in spite of no support from their communities of faith.

The people who were interviewed gave many stories of Christian giving. But they were not only stories about giving money or giving one's time for community volunteering. There were stories of people giving by doing their daily work with great skill and sensitivity. There were stories of doctors and teachers who were not only highly skilled in their work, but who also had a warm relationship with the people they served. One woman, Barbara, told of her father, a deliveryman. While she knew him at home as a loving parent, she never gave much thought about his job. In fact, she confessed, when she was in high school she was somewhat ashamed to admit that her father drove a delivery truck. Yet when he died she was astounded to learn of all the people he had served. He had listened to problems, loaned people money, helped them with chores, and always, always encouraged those who were down. They said that he gave them hope. His funeral was an event Barbara will never forget.

God's faithful people are givers. That is clear. One cannot acknowledge the grace of God in one's life without responding by giving to others. Yet, we must confess that Christian giving in God's world has been diminished by, of all things, the Christian church.

NINE

JUSTICE

Mr. Diehl, how can you possibly say you are a Christian and yet continue to work as an executive for a large corporation in the business field? That question has been put to me directly by more than one student as I have lectured on seminary campuses. It has been inferred more tactfully by many others who are in full-time church occupations. I have heard it in some form from pastors, from nuns and brothers I have worked with at the Interfaith Center for Corporate Responsibility, and from various executives of national denominational offices.

Behind the student's question is an assumption. Stated in its most simplistic form, it is "Christians are good and business people are bad." Christians stand for justice; business is unjust. Christians care about people; business executives care only about profit. Christians have integrity; people in business do not.

As one who has spent most of my life as an active member of my church and as an active businessman, the student's question is naturally a disturbing one for me. It is disturbing because it betrays some bad theology, and it is disturbing because it implies that justice is easily carried out in this complex world in which we live.

From a theological standpoint, the question suggests that Christians are to stay removed from those arenas of life which are perceived to be sinful. It implies that there are parts of God's creation which are to be written off by "loving Christians." Yet the psalmist reminds us that "the earth is the Lord's and the fulness thereof, the world and those who dwell therein" (Ps. 24:1), and Jesus claimed, "I came not to call the righteous, but the sinners" (Matt. 9:13). One should note, in passing, that it was the religious leaders of his time who were most critical of Jesus' association with undesirable people.

From a justice standpoint the question suggests that our social and economic structures operate so simply that anyone with a sense of Christian morality can easily perceive what the just action to take is in any given situation. It is this assumption that is most irritating to those business associates of mine who do struggle to connect faith to daily life.

During the interviews I conducted it became apparent that faithfulness involves a keen sense of justice. One should strive to do the "right thing" or to act as Jesus would want one to act. One should be aware of those who are being hurt by injustice and should work to correct the situation. One should have integrity, be honest, be truthful. These were the kinds of words I heard. Two people quoted the same section from Micah: "And what does the Lord require of you? to act justly and to love mercy and to walk humbly with your God" (Micah 6:8). John spoke with admiration of a business associate of his who tried to correct what he felt was an unethical practice within the company and then resigned when he was unable to do so.

It is for good reason that justice is seen as one of the attributes of God's faithful people. The Bible has much to say on the issue. The books of Moses in the Old Testament provided God's people with many rules designed to ensure a just society. The laws covered all aspects of life, including economics. In fact, a bit of business ethics is proclaimed in Leviticus where we read, "You shall do no wrong in judgment, in measures of length or weight or quantity. You shall have just balances, just weights" (Lev. 19:35–36). Justice was demanded of judges and officials in Deuteronomy: "You shall not pervert justice; you shall not show partiality; and you shall not take a bribe, for a bribe blinds the eyes of the wise and subverts the cause of the righteous" (Deut. 16:19). There are many admonitions to help the poor and powerless. "Give justice to the weak and the fatherless; maintain the right of the afflicted and the destitute. Rescue the weak and the needy; deliver them from the hand of the wicked" (Ps. 82:3–4). "And if your brother becomes poor, and cannot maintain himself with you, you shall maintain him; as a stranger and a sojourner he shall live with you" (Lev. 25:35). The prophets thundered out with calls to justice. "This is what the Lord says: Do what is just and right. Rescue from the hand of the oppressor the one who has been robbed. Do no wrong or violence to the alien, the fatherless or the widow" (Jer. 22:3).

One of the chief injustices Jesus sought to correct was that which came from a slavish legalism that ignored love. On several occasions he broke Sabbath laws in order to demonstrate the higher law of love. And it is interesting to note that he frequently confronted the scribes and Pharisees, the leaders of the church, for being hypocrites in their own treatment of the laws. "Woe to you Pharisees! for you tithe mint and rue and every herb, and neglect justice and the love of God; these you ought to have done, without neglecting the others. . . . Woe to you lawyers also! for you load men with burdens hard to bear, and you yourselves do not touch the burdens with one of your fingers" (Luke 11:42, 46). "Beware of the scribes, who like to go about in long robes, and to have salutations in the market places and the best seats in the synagogues and the places of honor at feasts, who devour widows' houses and for a pretense make long prayers. They will receive the greater condemnation" (Mark 12:38–40).

JUSTICE IN OUR SOCIETY

What about justice today? Do we live in a just society? Of course not. As Christians we confess that we have a sinful nature; that is, our basic instincts are to put ourselves first and God's concern for creation second. We acknowledge that we can never achieve perfection. God alone is perfect. Yet, God's faithful people also acknowledge that we are in a relationship with our Creator and as a response to God's graceful and unmerited acceptance of us, we are called to help make God's will be done on this earth.

It is surely not the will of God that millions of God's children live close to starvation in a time when the world has the ability to feed all its people adequately. It is surely not the will of God that 20 percent of all children born in the United States today are born into families in poverty. Or that 45 percent of all black teenagers are unemployed. Or that hard-working steelworkers and farmers have lost everything, including their self-respect, through no fault of their own.

It is true that we can never achieve perfection, but things certainly could be better than they are. And just as the prophets of old called for things to be better, the church, through its people and its leadership, has the duty to keep calling all of us to make things better.

The business community represents a readily identifiable starting point for making things better. The business community is a major participant in a global economic structure in which there are tremendous disparities between wealth and poverty. Knowing of the pervasiveness of self-interest and knowing of the economic power of persons, organizations, and nations, it is very inviting to claim that business people cannot possibly be Christians.

Evidence of greed and arrogance abound in the business community. Daily, it seems, we read of the overbilling of defense contractors, of corporate raiders, of insider trading on the stock market, of the laundering of illegal money by respected banks, of defective products in the marketplace, of toxic-waste disposal in residential areas, of hazardous working conditions, of price fixing, of false advertising, of tax evasion, of discrimination in the workplace, of bribery, embezzlement, arson, theft, and even murder, all within the framework of doing business in America today. It is not possible to read an issue of the *Wall Street Journal,* that champion of American business, without finding at least one news story related to one of the above evils. You do not need to get *Mother Jones* to learn about it. It is right there in the *Journal.*

It would be absolutely wrong, however, to conclude that all people in business would, given the opportunity, commit or condone these evils. I am convinced that the vast majority of people in business today are honest, decent people who are embarrassed by the misdeeds of a few. I believe most people in business want to do the right thing, to be just.

Furthermore, it is wrong to conclude that all of the wrongdoing in business today is intentionally committed by persons with evil motives. Stupidity, misjudgment, poor management, and bad luck are factors not uncommon in the business community. Moreover, there are times when no matter what is done, someone gets hurt. Many times a decision maker must choose what he or she perceives to be the lesser of two evils.

Any ethical problem involves values, responsibilities, and desired outcomes. The implementation of an ethical decision involves a strategy. All four of those factors—values, responsibilities, desired outcomes, and strategies—can be seen in different ways by different people.

Take the example of plant closings, which has been a popular topic in this country in recent years. As manager of sales for Bethlehem Steel a number of years ago, I participated in the decision as to whether one of our shops should be closed permanently. The plant had been a marginal one for many years. We had done everything we could to make the plant's costs competitive, but we were working against several obstacles peculiar to that facility. When demand for its products was high, it made money; when the demand was low, it lost money. It seemed to go in four-year cycles. At the time we considered closing the plant it had just finished a second straight year of substantial losses. Our other plants in the East which did similar work were limping along also, barely keeping in the profit column. In fact, at the time the entire corporation was losing money and all departments were pressed to review the viability of their individual operations.

I worked closely with our manager of shop operations, our market analyst, and the accountant assigned to our department. To close the shop permanently would mean the loss of about forty jobs, the loss of tax revenue to the community in which it operated, the loss of a nearby production point for our customers in that region, and the loss of business to competing shops in the area. To keep the shop open probably meant a continued loss of money to the company for some unknown duration. Furthermore, by closing the problem shop and by transferring its business to other shops of ours in that region we would be able to increase their volume and ensure their viability. Lots of values are involved here, and the four of us saw the values somewhat differently. Furthermore, our responsibilities differed. The production manager was responsible for profitable operations. He saw the value of closing the losing shop and transferring its work to the other nearby shops, thereby increasing their chances of staying alive. As sales manager, I was responsible to my management and to our customers. I saw that closing the shop would affect our customers and ultimately lose us future business. The accountant cared only about one thing: the fastest way to show profit. Our market analyst, who was familiar with business cycles, saw the value of possibly waiting another year to take advantage of the upswing he was forecasting for our business.

We had different values and had different responsibilities. We even had different desired outcomes. The accountant wanted a quick fix, no matter what it was. The production manager wanted a long-term viability for all the shops. I wanted maximum long-term sales participation in that region. The market analyst wanted to ensure that our capacity related to the demand he foresaw. What about the workers? In those days they were not a part of the decision-making process, and that was unfortunate. In recent years, the workers have been brought into such decisions more frequently. But we felt we were fully aware of the impact of our decision on them and, at one point in our discussions, I asked the question of how much of a factor was our obligation to them. Many of them had worked for us for years. Did we not owe them some extra consideration? Heads nodded. "Can we quantify it?" I asked. The accountant snapped back, "No way! My responsibility to management is to grind out the numbers and there is no honest way to factor in loyalty to employees."

Our values, our responsibilities, and our desired outcomes differed. So did our strategies. One wanted to close immediately. Others wanted to hang on for a year. We compromised. We took the shop down to a temporary closing status and put all but a couple of maintenance people on layoff. Those on layoff collected their supplemental unemployment insurance which, together with their state unemployment insurance, gave them almost full wages for a year. By not closing the shop permanently, we continued to lose money there, although at a lesser rate. The understanding was that we would maintain this status for a year at most. If the volume of business did not improve, we agreed to close the facility permanently at the end of the year.

Business did not improve and we closed and sold the shop the following year. Was our decision a good one? Depends upon your values. From the stockholders' position it was not good to have waited a year. And yet, it might have been if the market forecast had been right. From the position of all our workers, it was a good short-term decision. Those on layoff for a year got almost full wages, and those in our other shops got the extra work from our closed facility and thus were assured of continued work. The customers in that area and the local community saw it as indecisive management. We lost many of them. You decide.

The point of all this, however, is that each of the four of us sincerely felt we were acting ethically. Although the accountant may come across in this story as the hard-hearted guy, it is true that his responsibility was strictly to try to find as quick a way as possible to return to profitability. To temper his position with a concern for customers or employees or long-term business prospects would have been, in his mind, professionally unethical.

Having gone through a plant-closing decision myself, I can be somewhat sympathetic with others who must face the same issue. No one wants to cause people to lose their jobs. But it is entirely possible that, in order to save many jobs in a marginal company, it is necessary to eliminate those jobs where the organization is losing most of its money. What is most troubling to me, however, is the propensity of many managers today to be more concerned about short-term profitability than long-term viability. Business does have cycles and many older corporations can look back on years when they took heavy losses, only to return to profitability sometime later. In today's quick-fix environment, any quarter-year in which there is a loss is considered unacceptable and far too many plants are being closed in order to prevent the flow of red ink or even to prevent a drop in profitability. There are many and complex reasons for this situation, but one really does have to ask if enough concern is going into the human and social impact of so many plant closings.

INFLUENCES ON ETHICAL
DECISION MAKING

In doing the survey of business executives, I did not see much point in asking them to rate themselves on degree of ethics. Most of us would give ourselves high marks on that. Rather, we sought to find out which factors were most influential in shaping the decision making of the executives. We asked them to rate ten factors as being either very important, important, of little importance, or not important. The factors were "company policy," "ethics of my colleagues," "ethics of my competitors," "laws of the land," "need to produce

results," "opinions of others," "personal code of ethics," "professional code of ethics," "religious training," and "wishes of my
superiors."

In first place, with 69.8% of the executives saying it was very
important, was "personal code of ethics." Another 29.7% said it was
important. That is a total of 99.5%, which makes it a clear winner.
In second place was "laws of the land" with 43.2% listing it as very
important and 50.3% saying it was important.

Very close behind was "religious training" with 40.7% calling it
very important and 52.9% saying it was important.

"Professional code of ethics" won the fourth spot with 35.5%
saying it was very important and 50% calling it important.

In fifth place was "company policy" with 30.2% and 54.7%
respectively. From there on there was a substantial drop in the very
important column, with "need to produce results" scoring 12.3%,
followed by "ethics of my colleagues," "wishes of my superior,"
ethics of my competitors," and "opinions of others."

When we looked at that group who feel they have been called by
God in their present occupation, "personal code of ethics" is again
in first place, although somewhat higher than with the group as a
whole. This group gave a significantly higher importance to "religious
training," with 60% saying it was very important and 35.4% listing
it as important. On the other hand, "company policy" was given
less attention by this group than by the total, with only 21.5% listing
it as very important. This is an apparent example of the kind of
liberating freedom that will be discussed in the next chapter.

In response to other questions in the survey, very few of the
respondents agreed with the statement "I make my ethical decisions
on my job independent of my religious convictions." In response to
the statement "There are times in one's job when higher ethics or
religious principles must be put to one side for the sake of the
organization, provided one does not violate the law," 27.7% disagreed
strongly and another 54.3% disagreed. Among those who felt called
by God in their occupations, 50.9% disagreed strongly and 37%
disagreed.

By a small margin, the respondents tended to agree that "people
tend to set higher ethical and moral standards for their private lives
than for their work lives." When it came to themselves, however,

they disagreed with the same proposition, feeling that they did not find it difficult to maintain the same ethical code for their work lives as they did for their personal lives. It reminded me of the surveys we did many years ago on the issues of fair housing. People told us that while *they* had no objection to integrated housing, they were quite sure their neighbors did.

I must confess that I am a bit skeptical about the degree to which religious training shapes the decision-making process of most American business people. There is no doubt in my mind that they sincerely feel that their religious values are shaping their ethical decisions, but we need to look at the breadth of the religious training upon which they are drawing.

I have done enough business-ethics seminars to know that for most business people the religious teachings they draw upon are the Ten Commandments and the so-called golden rule. And, from my experience, most of them cannot accurately list the Ten Commandments. This is not to belittle the importance of the Ten Commandments and the golden rule; would that all of us lived by these standards. But it does raise the question of how adequate these particular precepts are in shaping the ethical decision making that business people are called upon to deal with in a very complex social and economic structure.

For example, the attributes of forgiveness and compassion thread through both the Old and New Testaments. They are principles basic to our very understanding of our relationship with God. Michael Maccoby labels such attributes of forgiveness and compassion as traits of the heart and points out that since corporate work rewards qualities of the head instead of the heart, it is almost impossible to develop traits of the heart within the corporate system.[1] If this is true, and my own experience in corporate life bears it out, then how are the Christian attributes of forgiveness and compassion integrated into decision making? Drawing upon the golden rule is not enough, because the truth is that many of us cannot even forgive ourselves. In the seminars I conduct with business people we use some case studies in which the issue of forgiveness and compassion have to be addressed. The most frequent response I get from my business colleagues when we get into this area is, "Now look, Bill, you know very well a business cannot be run on mushy love." When we remind ourselves that the world of business management is still heavily populated by males whose macho instincts do not naturally move in the direction of the more nurturing attributes of compassion and love, it is doubly important that the church help business persons connect faith and the workplace.

If we are doing a weekend conference on issues relating to business, I always invite a theologian to be part of the staff. The theologian is not asked to do much advance preparation, but rather to come, listen to the discussions, and then raise appropriate theological perspectives that would apply. We have been fortunate to have some very bright professors of Christian ethics at our events. They have been open and honest with the business people. They seldom attempt to give solutions to problems; rather they point to theological affirmations that seem to relate to the issues being discussed. Because they neither condemn nor offer solutions, they are listened to very attentively by the business people. Our postconference evaluations almost always indicate that the theologian's contribution to the conference was a highlight.

But what fascinates me is how appreciative are these theologians for the opportunity to "do theology" in areas they have seldom considered before. They all indicate that the weekend experience has been very helpful in the work they do in training prospective clergy. And they confess that we have asked them to do theology in areas which have been scarcely touched by religious scholars. It is apparent to me that not only do business people need to spend time on how our Christian beliefs relate to ethical decision making in the realm of business and economics, but also our church scholars.

Even when church leaders do attempt to address ethical decision making in the business world, it is often in a critical manner and with insufficient or incorrect facts. It is no wonder that many business people have developed a knee-jerk reaction to almost any type of criticism coming from the pulpit or from national church leaders. They become very defensive and, at times, threaten to leave the church or withhold contributions. Frequently, the clergy are bewildered by such reactions.

But let us look at it from the eyes of a business executive: Scott Anderson arrives in town as the new production manager for Atlas Pharmaceutical Company. The family joins a church. When it is discovered that Scott is a businessman, he is asked by his pastor to serve on the finance committee of the congregation. No matter that he is a production manager and knows little about finances. He is also asked to serve as an usher from time to time. Once a year, he is asked to play a leading role in the annual drive for pledges for the forthcoming year. Because he is a corporate person, he is expected to be a leader in giving to the church. He does not attend Sunday church school because the topics do not interest him. He gets annoyed when the pastor refers to him as vice-president of Ace Drug Company. He is not a vice-president and there is no such thing as Ace Drug Company.

One of the products produced at Scott's plant is a new drug used to treat a virulent tropical disease. Like any powerful drug, this product has some undesirable side effects. But the company's extensive research indicates that the risk of death as a side effect is very low and, when compared to its great potential for saving lives, it is clearly a product to market. Although the drug is still undergoing lengthy tests by the U.S. Food and Drug Administration, the company has decided to sell the drug in foreign markets. In those countries that have approval mechanisms for new drugs, the product has been tested and approved for sale. Those countries that have no testing programs have authorized the product for sale anyway.

One weekend, Scott is surprised to see a lengthy syndicated article in the Sunday supplement of his newspaper "exposing" the unethical marketing tactics of American drug producers. Scott is surprised to see his company named as one of the culprits and that the miracle drug produced in his plant has caused innumerable deaths. The article points out that this product is being marketed in other countries even though it is illegal in the United States. He is upset about the labeling of his product as being "illegal." It is technically illegal because the extensive U.S. testing program has not yet been completed, not because it is judged to be dangerous—as the article implies. But he is even more concerned about the report of "innumerable deaths." The next day he checks with the world headquarters' office of Atlas Pharmaceuticals and discovers that they have already checked into the article and discovered that the deaths were due to an entirely different drug, produced by a French company, but having a name similar to his product. The writer of the article had made a mistake.

The next Sunday, during the sermon, his pastor makes an extensive reference to the article and cites it as an example of the injustice of greedy Americans, marketing drugs in Third World countries knowing that they are too dangerous to be sold here in the USA. Scott visibly shook when his pastor called it "murder for greed." As he left the service that day, he said, "Pastor, your story about the drug company was wrong. The drug you were talking about is made in my plant, but it did not kill people, as you say it did. Why didn't you talk to me before you put it in your sermon?" His pastor was flustered. "Gee, Scott, I didn't know it was your company. I just reported on what I read. It certainly was nothing personal."

And that is the way it goes much too often. Business people are asked to serve in roles in the congregation with little or no interest in what they are doing in their work lives. They are not affirmed in any way in their ministries in their jobs. It is as if the church has absolutely no interest in what they do during the week. They are convinced that they live in two worlds. But, every now and then, the church leaders speak "prophetically" about their world and it is too often in a critical manner and with bad facts. No wonder the business folk get angry.

Having said all that, however, I am also aware of the fact that much does go wrong in business. Illegal things are done and sometimes even murder. What many of my business associates would really like would be for the church to bless everything that is done in the name of business. That will not do either.

If there is to be justice done in the business world, if the Christian faith is to have any impact on decision making, then business people need to stop being so defensive and acknowledge that the present system needs to be improved. At the same time, church leaders need to relate better to their parishioners in business, to support them in their Monday ministries, to encourage them into theological discourse of the issues they are facing, and to speak out prophetically only after getting their facts straight.

We have dealt at length with justice in the economic arena simply because it is an area most frequently cited as one of great injustice. But God's faithful people work for justice in many other areas of life.

Over the years, Judy and I have participated in a number of different social movements. We progressed from the civil rights movement in the sixties, through the Vietnam War in the late sixties and early seventies, to the women's movement, and, the peace movement. Three things can be generalized about Christians reaching out for justice, based on our experiences over the past twenty-five years.

First, those faithful who decide to act in support of justice issues are truly wonderful, loving people. In all four of the movements mentioned above, we encountered all kinds of people with all kinds of special interests. There were labor unions, environmental groups, counterculture groups, political groups, poor people, Gray Panthers, veterans groups, and others. Yes, and in some of the movements there were communists and socialists. Each movement gathered its own coalition of interested parties. But in each movement we found people there who were responding solely out of their own Christian convictions. These were beautiful people. They were warm, friendly, sharing people. Many of them radiated an inner peace and certainly that was striking. They were easy to talk to, and were always offering to share some food with others. They were not hostile toward those who were standing in the way of the movement. Yet they were resolute in the feeling that they were called by their Lord to be present. These people were frequently mediators when confrontations between demonstrators and police or military got out of hand. Some of them went to prison, but they did so calmly and without rancor. One place you are sure to find God's faithful people is in the social movements.

A second generalization we can make about Christians participating in social movements is that the decision to act does not come lightly. It is so easy to be oblivious to injustice, or to assume it is someone else's responsibility to correct it. I have always believed in equal treatment for all our citizens. And I recall that, in the 1950s, I was somewhat aware that blacks were not receiving equal treatment by our society. But it did not become a compelling thing to me until I saw blacks being beaten by police as they tried to integrate public bus stations and until I tried to secure housing for a black family wanting to move into our school district. Then the evil was clearly apparent and we joined the civil rights movement. Looking back, we should have been involved much earlier, but we just were not paying attention.

With the Vietnam War it was a matter of a complete reversal of position. Initially, I believed our intentions were right in Southeast Asia. I truly believed that we were out to help a nation seeking our assistance. And I still feel that our initial intentions were supportable, although perhaps naive. But along the way we lost our way. As the violence abroad and at home increased, so did our doubts. Kent State was the benchmark. When our own soldiers began killing our own college students, our own children, we knew it had all gone too far. We joined the movement. We, too, were among the throngs in Washington, in Harrisburg, and in our own hometown. Perhaps we should have seen the error of the Vietnam War much earlier. But we did not. We just were not paying enough attention.

A third generalization about acting for justice is that one is never quite certain about the strategies. And, unfortunately, we sometimes depreciate the Christian convictions of those who do not share our strategies. The peace issue is a perfect case in point.

I am convinced that no sane person is looking for a nuclear war. The question is, how do we avoid one? One strategy says that we maintain a clear superiority of arms so that no enemy can possibly destroy us without surely being destroyed. The other strategy says that because history has shown that nations which build vast military operations ultimately use them, the way to avoid nuclear war is to eliminate nuclear weapons. Within the nuclear disarmament strategy there are other substrategies. Unilateral reduction of weapons. SALT treaties. Moratorium on the testing of weapons. The peace issue becomes further complicated as we link other issues to the arms race—human rights; democratic self-determination; nonintervention in the affairs of sovereign nations. I agree with all these principles, yet as they become linked with the arms race, the priorities become confused. Is it worth risking a major war to rid a nation of a government which is friendly to another superpower?

I consider myself to be part of the peace movement but, as world events change, I have found my strategies changing and I wonder which one is best. And, more to the point, which strategy for peace is most clearly the will of God?

South Africa is another case in point. Assuming the United States has some degree of influence in South Africa, which strategy will most likely bring about the dismantlement of apartheid, which none of us supports? Should American companies get out or stay, hoping to be a tiny force for change? Should we try to persuade the South African government to take positive steps, or will sanctions force them to?

In so many instances, the pathway to justice is not clearly marked. We know what we want to achieve, but we are not sure of the right way to get there. Yet as God's faithful people we must act. So we study the issue, pray for guidance, make our best judgment, and strike out for justice. We know that our strategies may be wrong, but we move ahead with the assurance that our loving God will either support us or forgive us.

But these have been the big, national justice issues. God's people are called upon to act for justice in the everyday affairs of people. Someone is being mistreated on the job or in the neighborhood. An organization to which one belongs excludes certain people from its membership. Barriers are erected to keep people out of certain neighborhoods. Jokes are told or fun is poked at individuals or certain groups. Policy decisions are made at local, state, or national levels that work to the disadvantage of the poor and powerless.

Sometimes we are so much a part of the social fabric that we fail to see the injustices. And, so, we need to help each other be more sensitive and alert to them. The Bible has much to say about justice. A concern about justice and the courage to speak and act on behalf of it are clearly attributes of the faithful.

T E N

NO OTHER GODS

Vince Lombardi, former coach of the Green Bay Packers, will long be remembered for his passion for excellence and his determination to win. Under his leadership, the football team from the little town of Green Bay, Wisconsin, became a legend in its time. Lombardi so inspired his players to focus on winning that they consistently turned in superior performances and were among the top teams in the league year after year. Lombardi summed up his philosophy by saying, "Winning is not everything. It is the only thing." During his years as coach and in the years following, Lombardi was a coveted speaker among business organizations. It was partly because of his association with the Green Bay Packers but, more important, Lombardi always delivered a rousing speech on the importance of winning. He applied to business the same approach he used in coaching football; everything centered around winning.

Ours is a very competitive society. Whether it be in sports or business or performing arts or the classroom or the Miss America beauty contest, it is very important that we win, that we be "number one!" It is in winning that we establish our worth.

In order to win in business, many men and women are working sixty to seventy hours a week. They are giving total allegiance to their companies and their careers. The job comes first. And when one thing becomes the totality of life, other things suffer and are hurt. Marriages fail. Children are either unwanted or placed in the hands of others much of the day. There is no time for establishing friendships. Community life is nil. Care of self is frequently neglected. For the few who reach the top, success often seems hollow. For the many who do not reach the top, life is a failure.

For many Americans, their god is success. Success is invariably measured by material wealth, personal popularity, or position of power or status in one's community. Success, it is believed, brings security. Failure is endless insecurity. Success, as measured by the world's standards, can indeed become one's god.

The seventh and final attribute that we found among God's faithful people is that they have no other gods. At first glance, it might seem that such an attribute should be expected among all who claim to be followers of Jesus Christ. But for many of us, there is a constant battle going on within our lives over which god it is in whom we put our ultimate trust.

What is a god? Martin Luther, in his Large Catechism, defines it thus: "A god is that to which we look for all good and in which we find refuge in every time of need. To have a god is nothing else than to trust and believe him with our whole heart."[1] Luther then goes on to give, as an example, the person who accumulates money and property in order to gain a sense of security. The god for such a person is money and possessions, because the person feels secure in the belief that they will keep him or her safe and happy.

Reference was made in an earlier chapter to the encounter of Jesus and the rich ruler. Jesus perceived that although the ruler very strictly obeyed all the Commandments, his ultimate security was in his wealth. To test this, Jesus ordered him to sell everything he had, give it all to the poor, and to follow him. In short, Jesus asked him to make a clear declaration of which god he depended upon for his ultimate security. The rich man could not give up his wealth, because he could not give up all that security.

It is Jesus' next words which are frequently misunderstood. For he said, "It will be hard for a rich man to enter the kingdom of heaven. Again I tell you, it is easier for a camel to go through the eye of a needle than for a rich man to enter the kingdom of God." The astonished bystanders then asked, "Who then can be saved?" To which he replied, "With men this is impossible, but with God all things are possible" (Matt. 19:23–26).

Money and possessions, of themselves, are not evil. It is the accumulation of wealth, for the purpose of gaining "refuge in every time of need," as Luther put it, that makes money and possessions one's god. The psalmist warns, "If riches increase, set not your heart on them" (Ps. 62:10). Saint Paul taught that it was the love of money which was the root of all evil, and it is not only the wealthy who are capable of loving it. Often, those who have it least love it most. Yet no amount of money can bring security. As everyone knows, there is no way in which wealth can provide one's entry into the kingdom of God. Indeed, it *is* easier for a camel to go through the eye of a needle than for someone to gain entry into the kingdom of God through the accumulation of wealth. Yet Jesus reminds us that "With men this is impossible, but with God all things are possible." It is God who brings God's faithful into God's kingdom, whether they have wealth or not. But it is wealth, when loved for its own sake, which replaces God as our "refuge in every time of need."

Jesus is very clear about what must come first in one's life. He said,

> Therefore I tell you, do not be anxious about your life, what you shall eat or what you shall drink, nor about your body, what you shall put on. Is not life more than food, and the body more than clothing? Look at the birds of the air: they neither sow nor reap nor gather into barns, and yet your heavenly Father feeds them. Are you not of more value than they? And which of you by being anxious can add one cubit to his span of life? And why are you anxious about clothing? Consider the lilies of the field, how they grow; they neither toil nor spin; yet I tell you even Solomon in all his glory was not arrayed like of one these. But if God so clothes the grass of the field, which today is alive and tomorrow is thrown into the oven, will he not much more clothe you, O men of little faith? Therefore, do not be anxious, saying, "What shall we eat?" or "What shall we drink?" or "What shall we wear?" For the Gentiles seek all these things; and your heavenly Father knows that you need them all. But seek first his kingdom and his righteousness, and all these things shall be yours as well. (Matt. 6:25–33)

Seeking God's kingdom first can be a very slippery thing. If one's relationship with God is not dependent upon what one does, then what does one *do* to seek God's kingdom? Søren Kierkegaard struggled with this question when he wrote:

> "Seek ye first God's kingdom and his righteousness." What does this mean, what have I to do, or what sort of effort is it that can be said to seek or pursue the kingdom of God? Shall I try to get a job suitable to my talents and powers in order thereby to exert an influence? No, thou shall *first* seek God's kingdom. Shall I then give all my fortune to the poor? No, thou shall *first* seek God's kingdom. Shall I then go

out to proclaim this teaching to the world? No, thou shall *first* seek God's kingdom. But, then in a certain sense it is nothing I shall do. Yes, certainly, in a certain sense it is nothing, become nothing before God, learn to keep silent; in this silence is the beginning which is, *first* to seek God's kingdom.[2]

Richard Foster puts it this way with respect to seeking first the kingdom of God: "Nothing else can be central. The desire to get out of the rat race cannot be central, the redistribution of the world's wealth cannot be central, the concern for ecology cannot be central. The only thing which can be central . . . is to seek *first* God's kingdom and the righteousness, both personal and social, of that kingdom. Worthy as all other concerns may be, the moment *they* become the focus of our efforts, they become idolatry. . . . And, in fact, when the kingdom of God is genuinely placed first, ecological concerns, the poor, the equitable distribution of wealth and many other things will be given their proper attention.[3]

SIMPLICITY OF LIFE STYLE

When one is genuinely placing God first in one's life, then there is a style of living which is clearly an attribute of faithfulness. Simplicity borne of liberation is perhaps the most apparent element of this life style.

This simplicity of life style is not a self-imposed form of penance or even a form of asceticism. It is the natural consequence of ridding oneself of the gods of materialism, status, and power. Those who *first* seek the kingdom of God are very liberated people.

Jesus certainly had a simple life style. He did not renounce material possessions; his parables were filled with them. The lost coin, the lamp, the seed, the sheep, and many others. He frequently made the steward, the one who cares for the possessions of another, the central figure in his illustrations. But, although he did not renounce possessions, there is no evidence that he possessed any more than the basics for himself. Moreover, when he sent out the twelve (Luke 9:1–6) and the seventy (Luke 10:1–12), he instructed them to "carry no purse, no bag, no sandals" (Luke 10:4). You cannot travel any lighter than that!

The attractiveness of simplicity is not confined to faithful Christians, by any means. In their book *In Search of Excellence*, Peters and

Waterman devote an entire chapter to the way in which simplicity of form and function within corporations can contribute greatly to an organization's success. In art, music, and nature it is frequently the simple form that has great appeal. Some of life's most precious memories relate to simple events and experiences. For God's faithful people, "It's a gift to be simple, it's a gift to be free," as goes the old Shaker hymn. And that gift manifests itself in a magnificent life style.

That joy is also a fruit of faithfulness was borne out by several questions in the survey. In response to the statement "Persons with a solid religious faith generally are more joyful in their working lives," 12.6% strongly agreed and another 64.4% agreed. Among those who felt called by God in their present occupation, 22.4% strongly agreed and another 69.4% agreed. It is true, when the gods of power and materialism and careerism are not dominating one's life, one is more joyful at work.

DEALING WITH FAILURE

It follows that when we first seek the kingdom of God, there is little fear of failure and, when it comes, it can be handled with grace. In the survey, 37.4% of the business people strongly agreed with the statement "People are better able to deal with failure if they have a good religious foundation." Another 56.9% agreed with the statement. That is a 94.3% positive vote. Among those who feel called by God, the response was even stronger: 49% strongly agreed with the statement and an additional 49% agreed, for an affirmative total of 98%!

The ability to deal with failure also contributes to the life style of God's faithful. When one is not afraid of failing, one is much more open to others and to change. Because they do not fear failure, God's faithful people willingly accept responsibility for it when it comes. In the business world of intense competition and high achievement, it is rather startling to encounter an executive who publicly acknowledges an error or misjudgment. The contrary is generally true. When mistakes occur within the organization, performance-driven people usually rush to absolve themselves of all blame. "C.Y.A." is an expression quite common within large organizations. The willingness of a Christian to acknowledge failure openly is one small way in which a witness can be made to one's faith.

Because they are not afraid of failure, God's faithful people, therefore, are risk takers. They are willing to risk rejection by reaching out to someone else in love or by talking to another about Jesus. They are willing to risk loss of personal acceptance by speaking up when friends or associates display prejudice against individuals or groups. They are willing to support an unpopular cause if they feel it is what God would have them do.

Jesus took enormous risks during his ministry. That he risked his life is obvious from the manner in which it came to an end. And although he had a mission to reach all people, he was willing to risk the disapproval of the religious community and the establishment by challenging their hypocritical practices and by associating openly with the social outcasts of his day.

Risk-taking Christians are not hopeless idealists who are out of touch with the sinful nature of society. But if it comes to the choice between the possibility of being "taken" by some slick con artist or the possibility of turning away from someone truly in need, they will willingly risk being made a fool.

Risk taking is a much-admired trait in business today. In fact, as our nation loses more of its industrial jobs, there is great encouragement for unemployed workers to risk starting their own businesses. Entrepreneurship is an admired word in all circles today. And it is the high-risk entrepreneurs who successfully carry out huge corporate takeovers who are the legends of our times. Carl Ichan, T. Boone Pickens, Victor Posner, and others, while feared by many corporate managers, are nevertheless admired by much of society simply because they are audacious risk takers. But there is a significant difference between the risk taking of today's corporate raiders and the risk taking of God's faithful people. Corporate raiders, despite some statements to the contrary, are inevitably seeking to benefit themselves, frequently at the expense of others. Christian risk takers are seeking to benefit others at the possible expense of themselves.

Victor is the president of a small, family-owned textile company. It was purchased by his grandfather in the early 1900s. A number of the plant's seventy employees are second- or third-generation workers. For many of the employees the company is a kind of extended family. Some still call their sixty-three-year-old president "Vickey" from the days when he was a little boy. Some ten years ago, Victor agreed to go into a partnership with a friend in a new type of venture. In order to raise money for the new business, Victor secured two large loans. For one, he offered the assets of his textile plant as security. The second loan, surprisingly, was unsecured, based solely on Vic's integrity.

Due to unforeseen events, the new venture failed and there were not enough assets in it to repay the loans fully. His banker advised Vic to quit the textile business and use its assets to repay the loan. The recommendation had special appeal since the textile industry itself was changing and, if Victor's company was to continue to survive, he would have to invest heavily in new equipment. In fact, the textile industry had become so volatile that there was no assurance that, even with an investment in more modern equipment, the plant would survive. It was mighty tempting to walk away from it all. It would be best for him and his family.

But Victor also had to think about his employees. Not only did they look to him for continued employment in a region of Pennsylvania already depressed, but also his plant was the major employer in the tiny town in which it was located. To quit the business would have a devastating effect on the town, and yet there was little likelihood that the company could be sold as an ongoing operation.

Vic decided to hang in with the plant. He sold some of his personal property to pay off part of the outstanding loan and put up everything he owned personally as collateral for paying off the rest of the loan and for buying new equipment for his plant. He is keenly aware of the high risk of his decision. If his plan works, the company will survive and seventy people will continue to work. If it fails, everything he owns will be lost.

When you talk to Victor about all this, he does not speak in heroic terms. He is a rather quiet and modest person. Naturally, he does not relish the possibility of bankruptcy, but you get the feeling that for him there never really was a big choice to make between saving himself and saving the jobs of his people. It apparently was obvious to Victor all along that his employees' welfare was worth any personal risk he would have to take. Of such is the risk taking of God's faithful people.

Because they are not afraid of failure and because they are willing to take risks, God's faithful people are open and forgiving. They are open to making new friendships, inviting strangers into their homes, welcoming the new neighbor, listening to new ideas, and considering all sides of a controversial issue.

Dave is a member of our congregation who goes out of his way to greet everybody he possibly can on a Sunday morning. Although he sings in our choir, he quickly appears in the nave following the worship service and moves among the crowd, shaking hands and greeting everyone he possibly can. It is apparent that people love it and Dave frequently admonishes the rest of us to be more friendly. I hesitate to copy Dave—because of high membership turnover in our congregation I'm never quite certain who is a new member and who is a visitor. So I end up greeting the old friends I know are members. I do not want to blunder or appear to be foolish. To which Dave replies, "Sure I make mistakes at times, but so I look foolish. So what? People are forgiving and they all love to be greeted."

People are forgiving. Such is the observation of a person who is also forgiving of others. When we are willing to accept failure in ourselves, we inevitably must be willing to accept the failures of others. God's faithful people work hard at differentiating between the sin and the sinner. While there are certain acts and behavior of which they do not approve, they are willing to grant forgiveness to those who commit such acts. Such, of course, was the style of Jesus. When the Pharisees brought to him a woman caught in adultery and asked him if she should not be stoned, he suggested that the first stone should be thrown by anyone who is without sin. After they all departed, Jesus forgave the woman but admonished her to leave her life of sin (John 8:1–11).

Moreover, Jesus was not a one-time forgiver. He preached continual forgiveness. When Peter asks if he should forgive a brother who sins against him "as many as seven times," Jesus responds by saying "I do not say to you seven times, but seventy times seven" (Matt. 18:22).

As I listened to the stories told in the interviews about faithful people, there were other words which surfaced to describe the life style of the children of God. Words like peace-loving and peacemaker. Joyful. Hopeful. Optimistic. Gentle. Thankful. The words reminded one of the "fruits of the spirit" which Paul describes in his letter to the church in Galatia. He wrote, "But the fruit of the Spirit is love, joy, peace, patience, kindness, goodness, faithfulness, gentleness, self-control" (Gal. 5:22–23).

It is true that when a person puts God first in one's life and renounces those other gods of materialism, power, prestige, and fame, a distinctive life style results. This is not a hypothesis. It is demonstrable. It has been observed and reported by those who were asked to describe the attributes of those people in their lives who they count as faithful. It is there.

ELEVEN

THE BARRIERS TO FAITHFULNESS

That there are barriers standing in the way of Christian faithfulness should come as no surprise. The world offers an array of tempting gods for one to follow: financial security, power, public acclamation, outstanding achievement in one's life, and others. Moreover, the world recoils from any kind of faithfulness in which people "strive to become more Christlike in their daily lives," as our definition puts it. Christ renounced the false gods and threatened the religious and social structures of his day by condemning the practices of their leaders. Christ is no less a threat to today's world. To have large numbers of people striving to be more like him in their daily lives is an unwelcome thought for those whose lives have been built on the worship of other gods.

It should come as absolutely no surprise, therefore, that in the world of business, as well as in so many sectors of society today, there is no encouragement for people to grow more Christlike in their daily lives. In fact, as we have pointed out, the subject of religion and spirituality is totally ignored in the plethora of business-success books which have been gushing forth from publishing houses in recent years.

What is surprising and shocking is the way in which the church has erected so many barriers to faith development among the people of God. Surely the church should not be against its people "acknowledging God's graceful relationship" with them, as our definition of faithfulness puts it. Yet the responses in this study indicate that precious little is being done to help people make that acknowledgment. Surely the church cannot be against its people growing more Christlike in their daily lives. Yet the responses in this study indicate that not only is there little support coming from the churches for this development in the faith, but also that there are powerful forces at work within the churches which sever the connection between faith and daily life.

As mentioned in chapter 1, dualism has plagued the Christian church since its earliest years. In those parts of the Christian church where dualism is actively preached, it should come as no surprise that people are not connecting the activities of their daily lives with their faith beliefs. After all, the spiritual world is good; the material world is evil. The world of the church is sacred; the world of business and government and entertainment is secular. A certain amount of this dualistic thinking can be found in almost every part of the Christian church today. Obviously it is much stronger among some denominations than others, but it exists in some degree everywhere. Dualism inevitably pulls God's faithful people away from active engagement in the world. As long as it persists there will be barriers for faith development among the people of God.

But the discouraging thing to observe is that even within those Christian communities where dualism is renounced, there are powerful disincentives for the engagement of God's people in the world as the ministers of Jesus Christ. First of all, while they may be publicly affirmed for their service in the life of the congregation, they are not publicly affirmed for their calling in daily life in the world. The survey done in connection with the writing of this book shows how crucial it is for one to sense a calling in one's occupation; it shapes one's total life. To acknowledge the ministry of lay persons within congregational life but not to acknowledge their ministry in the world is to provide a disincentive for the latter.

Second, the study indicates that the kind of support provided by the church for faith development is not very relevant to the experiences of daily life. In terms of both content and style, Christian education programs focus almost exclusively on belief and ignore experience. Far too little attention is given to helping the people develop a life of personal prayer and meditation. While life in community is encouraged in a large congregational form, far too little encouragement is provided for the development of Christian community in small groups where there can be an active sharing of experiences. Christian giving is defined as giving to the church, not to the world. Justice is proclaimed in simplistic terms, not recognizing that there are highly complex problems which need careful study. And while there may be lip service paid to a Christian life style, very little is done to help people translate principles into practice in daily life. All of these influences tend to discourage faith development among the people of God.

There can be a variety of reasons for these disincentives to exist even within those Christian communities that renounce a dualistic view of life. Part of it may be traced to the nature of all institutions which share that demonic tendency to have the people serve the corporate needs rather than having the corporate body serve the people's needs. Part of it can be traced to pastors and other church leaders for whom the church is the center of the universe and who have little knowledge of or affinity for the world beyond the walls of the church. They may be totally ignorant of what needs to be done to help their people mature in the faith. Part of it is undoubtedly due to the many members of the churches for whom a separation of faith and daily life is desired since it permits them to enjoy the comfort of a religion that avoids the reality of the world about them.

PERSONAL EXPERIENCE

There is another factor, however, and I believe that by dealing with it, great progress can be made in lessening the other disincentives uncovered in this book. That factor is a lack of encouragement for the personal experience and expression of faith. In the seventy interviews I conducted, there were many stories of how the people lived out their faith in daily life experiences. Not one individual described a faithful person simply in terms of what they believed intellectually. No one said, "John is a faithful person because I know he truly believes in the Ten Commandments, the Apostle's Creed and the Lord's Prayer." If reference was made to the Ten Commandments it was with respect to how a person was trying to apply a commandment to a particular situation in their life. While it was implicit in these stories that people believed in the triune God, the validation of such belief always came in the form of real-life experiences in which the presence of God, Jesus Christ, or the Holy Spirit was felt. And the various petitions in the Lord's Prayer had meaning insofar as they related to particular situations in that person's world.

Will Boyer's definition of faithfulness was "belief in Jesus Christ and the action to back it up." Bill Romeiser said that a faithful person "demonstrates an adherence to belief in the face of problems or adversity." Over and over again, I heard words such as "caring," "loving," "relating," "forgiving," "sharing," "helping," "giving," and many others. They all boil down to experiencing. Experiencing the faith. Paul Tillich has much to say about experiencing the faith. His statement, quoted in chapter 2, that "there is no faith without participation" was exactly what I was hearing from the people I interviewed.

In his book *Hunger for Experience*, John E. Biersdorf reports on a study financed by the George D. Dayton Foundation in the early 1970s. The objective of the study was to determine why the mainline or "liberal" denominations were experiencing a malaise while the more fundamental denominations were demonstrating vital functions. At the risk of summarizing the study too briefly, the conclusion was that people need to experience their faith and that the conservative or fundamental denominations have tapped into that need. Biersdorf writes, "We do believe, however, that liberal churches have neglected personal religious experience and discipline. And we believe that this neglect of an essential aspect of faith has contributed to the institutional distress and self-doubt of the liberal churches."[1] Biersdorf says, "People today hunger for the experience of reality out of which life's meaning may come, not for *discussion* of reality."[2] I contend that our churches, at best, are still leading the people in the *discussions* of reality, not the experiences.

Biersdorf suggests that liberal Protestantism seems to fear that the hunger for experience, if dealt with, will lead to a "new pietism." "Piety." That word has not been used once in this book simply because it is still so much out of favor in our mainline denominations. Out of a fear that personal piety will develop into individualistic religion, many American denominations have been careful not to encourage it. Faith development in those churches has suffered as a consequence. Perhaps we need to learn that "piety" is not a dirty word.

Mention was made in an earlier chapter of a report prepared for the Religious Education Association of the United States and Canada by Dr. Constance Leean, which offered some important insights into faith development among adults. One of the thirteen major findings of the report was "involvement in and participation in a religious community *per se* is not a determining factor in one's growth in faith unless that community helps to 'sponsor' or encourage one's spiritual quest." The distinction between what is "religious" and what is "spiritual" deserves a great deal more study, suggests Leean, since in another of the major findings it was discovered that most of the people, "regardless of whether they are active members of a religious community, see themselves as more spiritual than religious."[3] The report indicated that personal apprehensions of God or a sense of the Holy were more prominent for most of the people surveyed than were corporate expressions of creeds or rituals or dogma. The report states, "Many people talked about how their faith has been strengthened through prayer and meditation, honest talks with friends, transforming moments, simple beauties in nature, certain works of art, challenging books and stirring pieces of music."[4] In the concluding recommendations, Leean points out that the religious communities have a great opportunity and challenge to nurture and support the unfolding of an authentic faith among their members. "Rather than be dismayed over the growing personalization of religion," she writes, "religious communities ought to align themselves with people's spiritual quests and complement this 'seeking' by offering an historical, theological and communal context for such explorations."[5]

So say I. In the past thirty-five years, our family has been a member of six different congregations in various parts of the country. That we believe passionately in membership and service within an organized religious community has been demonstrated by the decades of active participation by Judy and me in congregational, district, and national structures. We, in turn, have found lasting friendships through these associations and we have grown in our faith as the result of skillful teaching and preaching and through the reception of the holy sacraments.

However, our religious communities of faith generally did not provide for our growth in faithfulness in many other areas. My "acknowledgment" of my calling came not through my congregation, but through the reading of such authors as Hendrik Kraemer, Elton Trueblood, and Mark Gibbs. My growth came more from a broad range of books by William Stringfellow, Keith Miller, Dietrich Bonhoeffer, Paul Tillich, John A. T. Robinson, Reuel Howe, Elizabeth

O'Connor, Paul Tournier, Collin Morris, and Reinhold Niebuhr than from any educational programs in our congregations. Not one of these writers came to my attention through the Christian education program of our congregation. None of our churches had small support groups in existence when we joined. We had to develop our own and, in several cases, without the approval of the pastor. While I learned the importance of tithing in our little church in Detroit, it was not until I became involved as a volunteer with community human service organizations that I realized the full extent of Christian giving. And when Judy and I made our first significant stand on a justice issue by working for open housing on the Main Line of Philadelphia, we received a hostile reaction from a number of the members of the church council on which I served.

Does all this sound angry? Well, in a way it is, because I believe that the church of Jesus Christ is capable of doing far better than our records show. I believe that any congregation which has as its sole objective to get its members in the pews each Sunday morning and to get enough of them to support the programs of the congregation with time and money and does nothing else for the personal spiritual development of its people is in a class with the church in Laodicea. It was neither hot nor cold and therefore *deserved* to be "spewed out of my mouth" (Rev. 3:16).

At the same time, we have to acknowledge the responsibility of individual Christians to be agents of their own renewal. My experiences of being let down by my congregations is not unique. Hundreds of thousands of others have experienced the same thing and have used their own resources to grow in faithfulness. When one looks at some business people who relentlessly pursue self-development programs to advance their careers, yet remain virtual biblical illiterates, it is hard to place the full blame on the church. We are responsible people and we need to help ourselves and the church to nurture faithfulness. Where do we begin?

ACKNOWLEDGING OUR MINISTRY

Having done the survey of business persons, I have become convinced that a critical element of faithfulness is the acknowledgment of our relationship. Acknowledgment is more than understanding. When we acknowledge a message, we let the sender know that we have it. We respond. When the message is that, by the grace of God, we have been brought into a loving relationship with our Creator, through no merit of our own, and that we are therefore called to carry out the mission and ministry of Jesus Christ in this world of ours, we respond by declaring ourselves "priests of the Lord" and "ministers of our God," to take the words from Isaiah (61:6).

It is important to press the word "minister" upon all our people. Not only is it theologically appropriate, but it is an excellent teaching tool. It is universally accepted that our clergy have been "called" by God into the ordained ministry of a particular church or denomination. We need to use the same term, "minister," to provide convincing proof that all the baptized have been called into ministry of the church universal. I have had innumerable conversations with clergy who suggest that a better, less confusing term might be "disciple." That term is inadequate for the calling of the baptized. Check your dictionary.

As a member of the seventy-person commission that brought together three Lutheran bodies into what is now the Evangelical Lutheran Church in America, I found it fascinating to observe how difficult it was for Lutherans to translate their historic doctrine of the universal priesthood into a church structure that really saw Christian ministry as the work of all the people, not just the ordained. Many clergy felt that to elevate the ministry of the laity was to lower the ministry of the ordained. They saw ministry as a zero-sum game. They honestly did not see the potential for dramatically multiplying ministry. While its constitutional documents do not necessarily guarantee a change in the way things will be done, the new Lutheran church has come a step closer to attaining a universal priesthood.

I do agree with those who say it is now time to abolish the term "laity." It sets people apart. Today we speak of the ministry of the clergy and the ministry of the laity. Yet the ministry of the church is the ministry of all the people. Are we approaching the point where we can declare that all the baptized are ministers and some of them have been ordained by a particular church?

The survey I conducted showed conclusively to me that when a person can "feel a sense of ministry" or "feel called by God" in one's occupation, the response is far more positive to other attributes of faithfulness. Whether the disciplines of the faith create the feeling of being called or vice versa, I do not know. They probably develop together. But what this does say is that our communities of faith must make very strong efforts to affirm the ministries of all the people.

It is not within the scope of this book to go into all the ways in which congregations can affirm the ministries of their members. But it needs to be done publicly and privately. In the same way we recognize the ministry of church-council members or choir members or church-school teachers or stewardship visitors during our worship services, we need to recognize the ministries of public officials and homemakers and public-school teachers and farmers and students and all the rest within the framework of worship. Public recognition can also be given through parish newsletters, bulletin boards, church directories, and the like. Our parish directory, for example, gives the name, address, phone number, and ministry of every member. Even students and retired persons are considered to be called into ministry.

The private recognition of ministry comes through trying to help people match their talents with the world's needs. Do we really want to ask a woman to serve on the altar guild if she is highly qualified to be on the board of a community-service agency? When we try to persuade someone to teach in the Sunday church school, do we consider that their talents might be better utilized by running for the local school board? As working people approach retirement, does the Christian community help them discover the options open to them for new ministries in their lives or do we let them drift? Do we spend time with our young people, helping them to see that their career choice, whatever it may be, will involve ministry? Is all of this too much to expect from the church? Not if we take seriously the words of the apostle Paul who, when writing to the church at Ephesus, points out that the function of the church leaders is "to equip God's people for work in his service" (Eph. 4:11–12 NEB). Not only is this a role for the local congregation, but it is easily doable.

STRUCTURING FOR MINISTRY

First, there needs to be in each congregation a standing committee on ministry. In the same way that most parishes have standing committees for worship, education, property, finance, and the like, there should also be a committee charged with the responsibility of overseeing the total ministry of the congregation. As part of its work, the committee on ministry would evaluate the degree to which staff and the other committees contribute to supporting the overall ministry of all the members of the congregation. What needs to be done within the worship and education programs of the congregation to better equip people for ministry? How can the staff be more effective in doing the same? What resources are needed?

Second, there should be maintained a personal ministry file for each member of the congregation. It can simply be a single sheet of paper which gives the experience, interests, and talents of the individual. From time to time, possibly every other year, two or three members of the committee on ministry would meet with each member to discuss the person's present ministries and to explore other possibilities. While participation in this program would not be considered a requirement for membership in the congregation, it would be encouraged just as much as members are encouraged to attend worship and provide financial support.

Business persons might resonate with this suggestion very well for it is not unlike the personnel practices within their own organizations. Each employee has a personnel file in which is kept all data relating to the person's activities and experiences within the company. In most companies there is an annual review in which each employee reviews his or her performance over the past twelve months in relation to the employee's abilities and objectives. While the congregational "ministry review" might not evaluate performance, it would help to match opportunities for ministry with the skills and interests of all the people.

Since many congregations are now using personal computers, it would be an easy step to create a congregational data bank of experience, interests, and skills of the membership. Such a congregation could then advise community agencies that it stands ready to offer possible candidates for needed positions in nonprofit, public, and even private organizations. When such requests do come in, members of the committee on ministry would again review the potentials for ministry with those individuals who surface as potential candidates to fill the need.

The data bank would also be available for filling the needs of the national church offices. If, for example, the national church proposes to issue a social statement on medical ethics, congregational data banks could immediately identify those persons with experience or interests in the topic. Some of these people would be called upon to help prepare initial drafts of the social statements, but all of them would be given the opportunity to review the drafts and comment upon them. In short, the church would be drawing upon the expertise of all its "worldly ministers" to help it draw up a social statement having high credibility.

What a tremendous opportunity awaits for the teaching and implementation of the ministry of all God's people simply by affirming it through public and private channels within the congregation!

EQUIPPING THE SAINTS

Once people have come to acknowledge that they are called and sent by God, there needs to be a variety of opportunities for them to grow in faithfulness. The congregation represents the most logical point for providing growth. As was pointed out in chapter 5, however, both national polls and the survey done for this book indicate that only a small percentage of adult members of congregations participate in the Christian education programs offered. And although those respondents who felt called by God to their occupations were more positive about their spiritual disciplines than those who did not feel called by God, there was almost the same small percentage of them who participated regularly in adult education programs. Evidently, the adult education programs being offered do not meet the needs of our people. Not enough is being done to help people make the connections between their beliefs and their daily lives. People are more interested in discussing the experiential dimensions of their faith lives than they are about discussing dogma. And, unfortunately, dogma, without the real-life connections, is what is too frequently served up in many adult educational programs. If the gospel is no longer related to the material and temporal aspects of our lives, it loses its vitality and passion.

Dr. Constance Leean observed the same need to make connections. She writes, "A significant implication of the fact that most people do not equate faith with a set of beliefs or dogma but instead see faith as relational and attitudinal opens the door for discussions of personal faith experiences."[6] But it is not happening within congregations. Leean reports, "A thread running through this study is that people within the context of their religious communities have not been encouraged to examine or discuss their faith experiences. This seems strange when you consider that faith and the faith lives of its members ought to be a central concern within religious communities."[7] In fact, she sighted significant evidence that the "unstated norms" within congregations tend to mitigate *against* supporting people in their faith journeys.

The nurturing congregation must be sensitive to the need for people to discuss their faith experiences with each other. It may be that the Sunday morning adult study period is not the best time and place for such sharing. But the creative congregation must then act to "sponsor" such other opportunities and occasions as retreats, small support groups, centers for study and reflection, and the like.

If the congregation is to become a place where faith development occurs partly through the examination and discussion of actual faith experiences, then our seminaries need to make some adjustments also. Teaching future church leaders theology and dogma by itself will not do. They will have to be taught how to relate the beliefs of the church to the experiences of the people. I have attended some "lay courses" offered by the seminaries and they are generally nothing more than boiled-down seminary courses. Some have been frightfully dull. But the chief problem is that it is up to the student to make the connections between the content of the course and the real-life application. On the other hand, I have been in conferences where the topic is some current issue of concern to the participants and where the theologian is called upon to provide the connections with the theology of the church. These sessions are invariably alive and exciting because they bring the doctrine of the church into the experiences of the people. It is this kind of training that is needed for future church leaders.

Biersdorf, in reporting on the study of why the mainline denominations are in a period of malaise, expresses a similar concern about the seminaries. He points out that the theologians' preoccupation with scholarship "has left the realm of religious experience largely to the charismatics, unregarded groups of mystics, followers of Eastern disciplines and, ironically, humanistic psychologists." He says that efforts to provide pastoral training for introducing religious experience into the lives of the congregations "are usually relegated to the 'practical' (i.e., inferior) side of seminary curriculum . . . and regarded with disdain by serious theologians and ethicists."[8] Biersdorf concludes his book with these words: "While theologians talk about how one can talk about the experience of God, a motley assembly of saints and charlatans in the culture has been experimenting with a variety of paths to the experience itself. Our hope is that the faiths of the Judaeo-Christian tradition may reclaim that part of their own heritage that speaks to the contemporary cultural need for experience."[9]

If the church has erected so many barriers to the faith development of God's people, how is it that, in a survey of 174 business people who are solid churchgoers, about 30% do feel called by God in their present occupation and do respond very positively in such spiritual disciplines as personal prayer, Bible reading, tithing, corporate and family worship, and the reading of current religious books and magazines? How have they overcome the institutional disincentives?

The answer can be found in a little sign that hangs on the walls of many corporate training offices. The sign says, "All development is self-development." It was apparent from the interviews that much faith development occurs apart from the institutional church. It can develop as one person shares faith experiences with another across a kitchen table, on an airplane, or during lunch in the faculty dining room. It can develop when one individual tells another he or she is being prayed for. It can develop when a person passes along a meaningful book to another. It can develop when one person invites others to join in a koinonia group. It can develop when one person asks others to join in support of some worthy cause. Faith development can occur when one individual decides to begin practicing some of the classic spiritual disciplines that have been important in the lives of God's people for past generations. All of these acts can be self-initiated. This is not to say, however, that the Christian faith can develop fully without a relationship with a corporate body of Christians. The 30% of business persons who responded positively in so many areas also were much more positive in their continued association with their church. It does offer evidence that the power of the Holy Spirit is able to overcome many barriers to faithfulness if one truly seeks after it.

Whether faith development happens as a result of influences from the church or outside the church, it cannot happen without experience. "There is no faith without participation!" thunders Tillich.

In the introduction to this book we asked the question, What has happened to Christianity as found in mainstream Protestant churches today? The answer is clear. By not connecting the teachings of the faith to the experiences of the faithful, our churches have become increasingly irrelevant in the shaping of American life and culture.

Yet the faithful are out there. Faithfulness can be found and the marks of the faithful can be observed. What glorious potential still awaits the Christian church in America if it can truly affirm, equip, and support all its members for all their ministries in all the world.

NOTES

INTRODUCTION

1. Thomas J. Peters and Robert H. Waterman, Jr., *In Search of Excellence: Lessons from America's Best-Run Companies* (New York: Harper & Row, 1982).

CHAPTER 1

1. Thomas J. Peters and Nancy K. Austin, *A Passion for Excellence: The Leadership Difference* (New York: Random House, 1985).

2. Eliza G. C. Collins, ed., *Executive Success: Making It in Management*, Harvard Business Review (New York: John Wiley & Sons, 1983).

3. Craig R. Hickman and Michael A. Silva, *Creating Excellence* (New York: New American Library, 1984).

4. David L. Bradford and Allan R. Cohen, *Managing for Excellence: The Guide to Developing High Performance in Contemporary Organizations* (New York: John Wiley & Sons, 1984).

5. Henry C. Rogers, *Rogers' Rules for Success: Tips That Will Take You to the Top by One of America's Foremost Public Relations Experts* (Boston: St. Martin's Press, 1984).

6. Heinz Weihrich, *Management Excellence: Productivity through MBO* (New York: McGraw-Hill, 1985).

7. "The Year's 50 Most Fascinating Business People," *Fortune* (January 5, 1987): 30–111.

8. Barbara Kallen, "Praying for Guidance," *Forbes* (December 1, 1986): 221.

9. Donald G. Jones, ed., *Business, Religion and Ethics: Inquiry and Encounter* (Boston: Oelgeschlager, Gunn & Hain, 1982).

10. Oliver Williams and John Houck, eds., *The Judeo-Christian Vision and the Modern Corporation* (Notre Dame, Ind.: Univ. of Notre Dame Press, 1982).

11. Charles Margerison and Andrew Kakabadse, *How American Chief Executives Succeed* (New York: American Management Association Publications Division, 1984).

12. "1985 Giving USA," *Independent Sector Update* (May 1986), 1–2.

CHAPTER 2

1. Paul Tillich, *The Dynamics of Faith* (New York: Harper Torchbooks, 1957), introduction.

2. Ibid., 1.

3. Ibid., introduction.

4. Ibid., 100.

5. Ibid., 59.

6. Rudolph Bultmann, *Faith and Understanding, I*, trans. Louise Smith (New York: Harper & Row, 1969); and *Existence and Faith*, trans. Schubert M. Ogden (Cleveland: World Publishing, 1960).

7. Karl Barth, "The Doctrine of the Word of God," in *Church Dogmatics* (Edinburgh: T. & T. Clark, 1936), 4:742.

8. Ibid., 764.

9. Søren Kierkegaard, *Fear and Trembling*, trans. Walter Lowrie (Garden City, N.Y.: Doubleday & Co., 1954), 49.

10. James W. Woelfel, *Bonhoeffer's Theology* (Nashville: Abingdon Press, 1970), 264.

11. Morris Ashcraft, *Rudolph Bultmann*, ed. Bob E. Patterson (Waco, Tex.: Word, 1972), 88.

12. Martin Luther, *Preface to the New Testament*, quoted in William Barclay, *The Letters of James and Peter* (Philadelphia: Westminster Press, 1976), 6.

13. Martin Luther, as quoted in Gerhard Ebeling, *Luther* (Philadelphia: Fortress Press, 1972), 40.

14. David L. Mueller, *Karl Barth*, ed. Bob E. Patterson (Waco, Tex.: Word, 1972), 84.

CHAPTER 3

1. *St. Paul Pioneer Press and Dispatch* (June 9, 1985).

2. Joseph Sittler, *Gravity and Grace: Reflections and Provocations*, ed. Linda Marie Delloff (Minneapolis: Augsburg Publishing House, 1986), 24.

CHAPTER 4

1. Thomas J. Watson, Jr., *A Business and Its Beliefs: The Ideas That Helped Build IBM* (Ann Arbor, Mich.: Books on Demand, n.d.), as quoted in Lawrence M. Miller, *American Spirit: Visions of a New Corporate Culture* (New York: William Morrow, 1984), 36.

2. Sittler, *Gravity and Grace*, 52.

CHAPTER 5

1. C. Samuel Calian, *The Gospel According to The Wall Street Journal* (Atlanta: John Knox Press, 1975).

2. Richard R. Gilbert in his foreword to Jones, *Business, Religion and Ethics*, vii.

3. Dr. Constance Leean, *Faith Development in the Adult Life Cycle* (New York: Religious Association Press, 1985), Module 2, 61.

CHAPTER 6

1. *How American Chief Executives Succeed*, 24.

2. Ibid., 26.

3. Thomas R. Kelly, *A Testament of Devotion* (New York: Harper & Brothers, 1941).

4. Richard J. Foster, *Celebration of Discipline: Paths to Spiritual Growth* (New York: Harper & Row, 1978).

5. John Baillie, *Diary of Private Prayer* (New York: Charles Scribner's Sons, 1978).

6. Leslie F. Brandt, *Meditations on a Loving God* (St. Louis: Concordia Publishing House, 1983); and *Epistles—Now* (St. Louis: Concordia Publishing House, 1976).

7. Frederick Buechner, *Now and Then* (New York: Harper & Row, 1983); and *The Hungering Dark* (New York: Harper & Row, 1985).

8. Michael Quoist, *With Open Heart* (New York: Crossroad, 1983).

9. Robert Raines, *Creative Broodings* (New York: Macmillan, 1966).

10. Salvatore R. Maddi and Suzanne C. Kobasa, *The Hardy Executive: Health under Stress* (Homewood, Ill.: Dow Jones-Irwin, 1984).

11. Mark Gibbs, *God's Lively People* (Philadelphia: Westminster Press, 1971), 78.

CHAPTER 7

1. Elton Trueblood, "Conversion Within the Church," in *The Yoke of Christ* (New York: Harper & Brothers, 1958), 53.

2. William E. Diehl, *Thank God, It's Monday!* Laity Exchange Books (Philadelphia: Fortress Press, 1982).

3. Findley B. Edge in his introduction to William Clemmons and Harvey Hester, *Growth Through Groups* (Nashville: Broadman Press, 1974), 17.

4. Ibid., 18.

5. Ibid.

6. Michael Maccoby, *The Gamesman, the New Corporate Leaders* (New York: Simon & Schuster, 1976).

CHAPTER 8

1. Bernice Kanner, "What Price Ethics?" *New York* (July 14, 1986): 28–34.

2. Myron Magnet, "The Decline and Fall of Business Ethics," *Fortune* (December 8, 1986): 65.

3. Robert N. Bellah, *Habits of the Heart: Individualism and Commitment in American Life* (New York: Harper & Row, 1986), 285.

4. Independent Sector news release, August 21, 1986.

5. Ibid.

6. Brian O'Connell, *Origins, Dimensions and Impact of America's Voluntary Spirit* (Washington, D.C.: Independent Sector, 1984), 2.

7. Brian O'Connell, *Update*, Independent Sector newsletter (September 1985).

8. John Hess, "Our Horn of Plenty Is Running Out," *Washington Post* (July 20, 1986).

CHAPTER 9

1. Maccoby, *Gamesman*, 178.

CHAPTER 10

1. Martin Luther, *The Large Catechism of Martin Luther* (Philadelphia: Fortress Press, 1959), 9.
2. Søren Kierkegaard, *Christian Discourses*, trans. Walter Lowrie (New York: Oxford Univ. Press, 1940), 322.
3. Foster, *Celebration of Discipline*, 76.

CHAPTER 11

1. John E. Biersdorf, *Hunger for Experience: Vital Religious Communities in America Today* (New York: Seabury Press, 1975), 121.
2. Ibid., 136.
3. Leean, *Faith Development*, 25.
4. Ibid., 41.
5. Ibid., 61.
6. Ibid., 61.
7. Ibid., 49.
8. Biersdorf, *Hunger for Experience*, 139.
9. Ibid., 140.